A Guide to English Grammar using Color Coding

This manual is dedicated to Bernie, Lori, Jon, and Gwen.

The King's English

The Color of English

Patricia Didden

Copyright © 2015 by Patricia Didden

The King's English
The Color of English
by Patricia Didden

Printed in the United States of America

ISBN 9781498458979

All rights reserved solely by the author. The author guarantees all contents are original and do not infringe upon the legal rights of any other person or work. No part of this book may be reproduced in any form without the permission of the author. The views expressed in this book are not necessarily those of the publisher.

www.xulonpress.com

Table of Contents

Introduction ix

Chapter 1: Parts of Speech 17

Chapter 2: How to Parse 88

Chapter 3: How to Diagram 121

Glossary 167

Introduction

"Baby Barred Owl" by Larry Kitchen

WHO, WHAT, AND WHY: AN INTRODUCTION:

Patricia Didden is the wife of retired pastor Bernard Didden and the mother of their three grown children. After rearing Lori, Jon, and Gwen, she joined the staff of Berks Christian School, Birdsboro, PA, where she taught secondary school English for twenty-five years. During this time she developed her color-coding method of teaching English grammar.

She has enjoyed a lifelong fascination with words. She likes to write short articles based on her observations of God at work in the world around her. She wrote a variety column, *Small World,* for the Reading (PA) *Eagle* for fifteen years.

She graduated from Bob Jones University, Greenville, SC, with a Bachelor of Science degree and from Kutztown University, Kutztown, PA, with a Master of Arts degree.

THIS IS WHY SHE WISHES TO SHARE HER COLOR-CODING METHOD WITH YOU:

"When I began teaching high school English at Berks Christian School, I noticed that the subject of grammar seemed too abstract for many students to understand. One day I realized that the eight basic colors could be assigned to the eight parts of speech. What would happen if I should assign a color (something one can easily visualize) to each part of speech?

"The students accepted this idea at once. Soon everyone had learned how to take apart and put together any sentence that I presented to them. They began to understand the various functions of the parts of speech. For example, by visualizing a cat in a blue box, they soon learned how to identify a prepositional phrase. By visualizing a green traffic light, they quickly learned how to spot the main verb in any sentence. They were on their way!

"Some years later, I read a biography of Winston Churchill. In this book, I learned that as a young man Churchill was hopeless at understanding the basics of English grammar. He was a student at Harrow, and he was 'going down for the third time' when Robert Somerville (a tutor who, according to the author, 'richly deserves at least a footnote in history') took him in hand.

"Somerville devised a system of *using colored pens* to identify the subject, verb, and object of long, complicated sentences. Churchill took to this daily drill at once. 'Thus I got into my bones the essential structure of the ordinary British sentence – which is a noble thing,' he later wrote.* Furthermore, he eventually became one of the greatest prose writers of our generation.

"No, I was not the first person to discover the idea of using color coding, but I certainly found it to be an effective learning tool!"

*Manchester, Wm. *The Last Lion – Winston Spencer Churchill –Visions of Glory 1874-1932*. Little, Brown, and Co: Boston, 1983.

Acknowledgements

From the start this project was a family affair. Our daughter Gwen encouraged me to document this method by saying, "Mom, I don't want you to take this idea to Heaven with you." Our daughter Lori, a calligraphist, designed the cover and dedication page. Our son Jon took care of phone calls, answering questions and taking down addresses. My thanks go out to the three of you.

Our grandson Christian Hernandez configured the diagrams, and my brother Larry Kitchen shared his nature photographs and took the picture for the last page. I thank both of you for your good work!

Thank you, Rochelle Musser, for introducing me to Sandrine Dorsainvil. Through tutoring her, I came to realize that the color-coding method is still a useful tool.

A special word of gratitude goes to the friends who gave me valuable technical assistance. They are as follows: Paulette Landis, Tom Organtini, and my brother-in-law Paul Brownback. Jean Grover walked side by side with me through the final phases; without her, this manual would not be a reality.

    Finally, I want to thank my husband Bernie and my brother-in-law Tedd Didden for their invaluable support, helpful suggestions, and constant faith in this project. You have my undying gratitude.

Endorsements for **The King's English** from former students:

"The King's English takes the pain out of learning English grammar...Simple, accessible language and visuals make this user-friendly book particularly invaluable to the ESL/EFL student."
– James B. Harr, English faculty, Wake Technical Community College, Raleigh, NC

"It was a great system that made a big difference in my understanding the mechanics of the English language."
– Bradley Fink, SGT, US Army Infantry

"You were an inspiring teacher. I learned my grammar and Shakespeare so well that I still dream about it!"
– Rachel Rebert, former student

"Using colors made diagramming sentences more fun! Twenty years later, I still remember the color we used for each part of speech."
– Chris Stoltz, Pre-K teacher

"As a visual learner and artistic student, the use of color-coding grabbed my attention. . .The skills I learned through this technique converted me into a grammar-lover, which encouraged me to pursue a college degree in English, a master's degree in publishing, and a career as a journalist and professional writer."
– Natalie Shaak, Communications Manager, Drexel University LeBow College of Business, Philadelphia, PA.

"Mrs. Didden's methods are successful by virtue of her creative and comprehensive style as well as her contagious passion for grammar. This system gave me the tools that set me up for success in my collegiate and professional careers. This program has been helpful to me as a foreign language learner as well."
– Kris Hoffman, missionary

Parts of Speech

"Hello World" by Larry Kitchen

WHAT SETS THE KING'S ENGLISH APART?

1. **The King's English** uses the eight basic colors to represent the eight parts of speech. This method takes the rules of grammar out of the **abstract** and gives them a **concrete** meaning.

2. Since color, like music, uses no language, there is therefore **no language barrier** to the use of **The King's English** method.

3. **The King's English** uses a few simple **memory hooks** and **mental pictures** to introduce the basic concepts of understanding English grammar.

4. **The King's English** is a hands-on manual. Most pages have **fill-in spaces** for you to use your colored pencils, and convenient **answer keys** appear next to the practice pages.

YOU WILL NEED THREE THINGS:

1. Before you begin working on The King's English, you will need to purchase a box of colored pencils or crayons. Make sure the eight basic colors are represented in your box.

2. You will also need a small pack of 3 x 5 unlined cards. As you progress, you will build a fund of basic knowledge. I will show you how to write out this information flashcard style on these cards. You will find them easy to carry with you in your pocket or purse. This way you will be able to review this information during free time.

3. Make sure you have a dictionary handy as you work. Any size or type of dictionary will be usable. All dictionaries list the part of speech next to every word. This is why you will often find a dictionary to be useful.

HOW TO USE *THE KING'S ENGLISH*:

Every single practice page that appears in this manual is followed by an **answer key**. This **answer key** is **not** provided in order **to see if you know the right answer.** It is provided **to show you the right answer**. It is there **to help you to learn this system**.

Please feel free to turn to the **answer key** the moment a question arises in your mind. Refer to the **answer key** as you supply your own answers. **The answer key is a learning tool**. I want you to use it as **a silent instructor** to help you understand grammar as you work your way through this book.

Use the dictionary to help you understand the parts of speech. Sometimes a pronoun becomes an adjective. At other times a helping verb will appear as a linking verb. Open you dictionary for clarification. All will become clear.

The King's English

Assigning Colors to Parts of Speech:

A **VERB** is a word that (1.) **shows** action, (2.) **links** a word to the subject, (3.) **helps** another verb, or (4.) **indicates** existence.

We use the color **GREEN** to mark out **VERBS**. With a traffic light **GREEN** means **GO**, and that's what verbs usually do – they go!

A **NOUN** is a word that names a (1.) **person**, (2.) **place**, (3.) **thing**, or (4) **idea**.

We use the color **YELLOW** to indicate **NOUNS**, because, like the sun – which is **YELLOW** and gives light – **NOUNS** also provide light in a sentence by explaining the **VERB**.

The King's English

A **PRONOUN** is a word that takes the place of a **NOUN**. Nominative Case Pronouns are: **I, you, he, she, it, we, you, they**. Objective Case Pronouns are: **me, you, him, her, it, us, you, them**.

We use the color **ORANGE** to indicate **PRONOUNS** because **ORANGE** is similar to **YELLOW** as **NOUNS** are similar to **PRONOUNS**.

An **ADJECTIVE** is a word that modifies (or describes) a **NOUN** or a **PRONOUN**. It answers the following questions: **what kind? which one? how many? how much, whose?**.

We use the color **RED** to indicate an **ADJECTIVE**, because **RED** is a bright decorative color that takes the eye at once; **ADJECTIVES** decorate **NOUNS** and brighten sentences as well.

The King's English

An **ADVERB** is a word that modifies (or describes) a **VERB**, **ADJECTIVE**, or another **ADVERB**. An **ADVERB** answers the following questions: **where? when? how? how often? how much?** (Hint: **ADVERBS** very often end in *ly*.)

We use the color **PURPLE** to indicate an **ADVERB**, because **PURPLE** is a **KINGLY** color, and the word *kingly* ends in *ly*.

A **PREPOSITION** is a word that shows how a **NOUN** or **PRONOUN** is related to the sentence. It **always** appears as the **first word** of a **phrase** (a **phrase** is a group of related words). A **PREPOSITIONAL PHRASE** always ends with a **NOUN**.

Visualize a cat and a box. Remember that the **PREPOSITION** can do anything the cat can do. **EXAMPLE**: The cat goes **to** the box, **over** the box, **under** the box, **beside** the box. Get the picture?

The King's English

A **CONJUNCTION** is a word that joins words or groups of words. **BROWN** is the color of rope, and rope ties things together as the **CONJUNCTION** ties words together. Memorize these conjunctions: **and, but, or, nor, for, yet.**

EXAMPLE: Emmeline **and** Marceline are friends, **but** each cat likes her own space.

An **INTERJECTION** gives **POWER** and **PUNCH** to a sentence. Often an exclamation point is added, as the **INTERJECTION** usually expresses strong feeling, such as **WOW!**

We use the color **BLACK** to indicate an interjection because **BLACK** is a strong color, just as an **INTERJECTION** is a strong word.

HINTS FOR RECOGNIZING PARTS OF SPEECH:

1. A VERB is a word that. . .

SHOWS ACTION: If you see a word in a sentence that answers the question, "Can I **DO** this?" that word will be an **ACTION VERB** **(AV)**.

EXAMPLE: The brown cow **chewed** her cud.

An **ACTION VERB** is always followed by a **direct object (DO)**. The **direct object** in our example is the word *cud*, a **NOUN**.

INDICATES EXISTENCE: This **VERB** is complete in itself; it needs no other word to further explain its meaning. This **VERB** is known as a **VERB INTRANSITIVE** **(VI)**.

EXAMPLE: The brown cow **slept.** Here we understand fully what the cow was doing; we need no other word to complete the meaning.

LINKS THE SUBJECT OF A SENTENCE TO A DIRECT OBJECT.

EXAMPLES: The cow **is** brown. The cow **was** a good milker.

MEMORIZE THESE EIGHT LINKING VERBS: am, is, are, was, were, be, being, been.

2. A NOUN is a word that **NAMES** a **PERSON, PLACE, THING, or IDEA.**

3. A PRONOUN is a word that takes the place of a NOUN.

These PRONOUNS take the place of the **subject (S)** in a sentence: I, you, he, she, it, we, you, they.

These PRONOUNS take the place of the **object (DO)** of the sentence: me, you, him, her, it, us, you, them.

4. An ADJECTIVE describes a NOUN or a PRONOUN. ADJECTIVES tend to cluster around NOUNS. It often takes more than one ADJECTIVE to describe one NOUN. The words *a, an,* and *the* (known as **articles**) are actually ADJECTIVES, too.

ADJECTIVES answer these questions: what kind? which one? how many? how much? whose?

5. An ADVERB describes a VERB, an ADJECTIVE, or another ADVERB. ADVERBS cluster around VERBS and often end in *ly*. ADVERBS answer these questions: where? when? how? how often? how much? to what extent?

6. A **PREPOSITION** introduces a **phrase** (a group of related words).

EXAMPLES: I've got the world (**on** a string), sitting (**on** a rainbow), got the string (**around** my finger. . .)

A **PREPOSITION** can do anything a cat can do as it moves toward a box: "The cat goes **around, over, under, above, into, near, toward, within, off, on, after, against, to, behind** the box."

7. A **CONJUNCTION** is a word that joins words or groups of words. Memorize these basic conjunctions: **and, but, or, nor, for, yet.**

8. An **INTERJECTION** is a word that expresses strong feeling. It gives a sentence **POWER** AND **PUNCH.**

Verb

A **VERB** is a word that (1.) **shows** action, (2.) **links** a word to the subject, (3.) **helps** another verb, or (4.) **indicates** existence.

We use the color GREEN to mark out VERBS. With a traffic light GREEN means GO, and that's what verbs usually do – they go!

Examples:

1. **Shows** action: Emmeline chased her tail.

2. **Links** the subject to a complement: Emmeline is a cat.

3. **Helps** the main verb make a clear statement: Emmeline will not be removed from her blue box. (will be removed is the verb phrase; the adverb *not* **explains** the phrase.)

4. **Indicates** existence: The tree grows.

HOW TO SPOT A VERB:

The hub of a wheel holds and directs the spokes. The verb is the hub of a sentence, connecting and directing the seven other parts of speech. **Therefore, find the action verb first.**

To do this, ask yourself this question as you look over the words: **could I do this**? **Could I walk, sleep, sneeze, cry, laugh**, etc? If you say "yes", you have a verb.

Then check for a *linking verb*. This type of verb does not express action; rather, it **links** the subject of the sentence to a word that **completes** the main thought (the general term for **this** word is **a complement**.) Now, in order to recognize the linking verb, you need to memorize the nineteen linking verbs. Are you up to that? Here they are:

am, is, are, was, were, be, being, been,
Taste, feel, smell, sound, look,
appear, become, seem, grow, remain, stay.

We use green to mark out a verb because, when you see a traffic light, **green means go!**

FIND THE VERBS AND MARK THEM IN GREEN:

The King's English needs a palace with a family who lives there, so I will take this opportunity to introduce a few of the family members to you. (By the way, the palace is named Greytowers.)

First, we have Queen Juliana. She is tall and blond – beautiful in a willowy, Scandinavian sort of way. She is very proud of her two daughters, and she is very careful to train them in the best manners of royalty. Queen Juliana owns a fluffy, white Persian cat named Emmeline. Persian cats are known for their serene temperament and dignified demeanor. These characteristics make Emmeline a perfect pet for the Queen. She is very proud to share the Queen's apartment. She just naturally tries to tell the other cats what to do. This, however, rarely works out in practice.

Next in line is the Queen's elder daughter Augusta Stephania. She goes by the nickname "Gussie". Her cat is a beautiful multi-colored Tortoiseshell named Marceline.

ANSWER KEY:

The King's English **needs** a palace with a family who **lives** there, so I **will take** this opportunity to **introduce** a few of the family members to *you*. (By the way, the palace **is** named Greytowers.)

First, we **have** Queen Juliana. She **is** tall and blond – beautiful in a willowy, Scandinavian sort of way. She **is** very proud of her two daughters, and she **is** very careful to **train** them in the best manners of royalty. Queen Juliana **owns** a fluffy, white Persian cat **named** Emmeline. Persian cats **are known** for their serene temperament and dignified demeanor. These characteristics **make** Emmeline a perfect pet for the Queen. She **is** very proud to **share** the Queen's apartment. She just naturally **tries** to **tell** the other cats what to **do.** This, however, rarely **works** out in practice.

Next in line **is** the Queen's elder daughter Augusta Stephania. She **goes** by the nickname "Gussie". Her cat **is** a beautiful multi-colored Tortoiseshell **named** Marceline.

FIND THE VERBS AND MARK THEM IN GREEN:

Marceline is a natural leader. She is constantly at work trying to "get one over" on Emmeline, and she often succeeds. Gussie sometimes calls her "Tortie" for short.

The queen's second daughter is named Vanessa Regina. Her nickname is "Nessa", and her cat is a grayish-black American Shorthair named "Smokey". (This is short for "Smoking Gun".)

Vanessa once read the following statement in a book on cats: "This breed is known for its longevity, robust health, good looks, sweet personality, and amiability with children." Smokey never forgot it. Smokey is very protective of both the princesses. He is also quite a recluse, often finding dark corners or large cushions in which to hide, especially if he sees company in the palace. Then he disappears, not showing up until dinner time. It is possible that Smokey thinks he is the main man in the family. This, however, is not true.

ANSWER KEY:

Marceline **is** a natural leader. She **is** constantly at work **trying** to "**get** one over" on Emmeline, and she often **succeeds**. Gussie sometimes **calls** her "Tortie" for short.

The queen's second daughter **is named** Vanessa Regina. Her nickname **is** "Nessa", and her cat **is** a grayish-black American Shorthair named "Smokey". (This **is** short for "Smoking Gun".)

Vanessa once **read** the following statement in a book on cats: "This breed **is known** for its longevity, robust health, good looks, sweet personality, and amiability with children." Smokey never **forgot** it. Smokey **is** very protective of both the princesses. He **is** also quite a recluse, often **finding** dark corners or large cushions in which to **hide,** especially if he **sees** company in the palace. Then he **disappears**, not **showing** up until dinner time. It **is** possible that Smokey **thinks** he **is** the main man in the family. This, however, **is** not true.

FIND THE VERBS AND MARK THEM IN GREEN:

King Constantine makes time in his busy schedule to spend with the girls at the end of each day. The girls both love and respect their tall, handsome father.

    The girls also have an older brother whom they both adore. His name is Sergio Paulo. Sergio is away at school for much of the year. He does, however, come home for frequent holidays. After each holiday, when Sergio leaves to go back to school, the girls begin at once to count the days until he comes home again. He is an avid scrabble player. The girls and Sergio spend many a lively evening playing scrabble. But Sergio's greatest love is foxhunting. His second greatest love is his spirited piebald pony Jack. He received Jack as a birthday gift when he was ten years old, and the two of them connected at once through their natural love of foxhunting. Jack learned quickly how to follow the fox, jumping over bushes and brambles and gullies and streambeds, ignoring stones or logs that might impede his progress. Sergio, being a natural horseman, only aided and abetted Jack in his wild progress.

ANSWER KEY:

King Constantine **makes** time in his busy schedule to **spend** with the girls at the end of each day. The girls both **love** and **respect** their tall, handsome father.

    The girls also **have** an older brother whom they both **adore**. His name **is** Sergio Paulo. Sergio **is** away at school for much of the year. He **does**, however, **come** home for frequent holidays. After each holiday, when Sergio **leaves** to **go** back to school, the girls **begin** at once to **count** the days until he **comes** home again. He **is** an avid scrabble player. The girls and Sergio **spend** many a lively evening **playing** scrabble. But Sergio's greatest love **is** foxhunting. His second greatest love **is** his spirited piebald pony Jack. He **received** Jack as a birthday gift when he **was** ten years old, and the two of them **connected** at once through their natural love of foxhunting. Jack **learned** quickly how to **follow** the fox, **jumping** over bushes and brambles an gullies and streambeds, **ignoring** stones or logs that might **impede** his progress. Sergio, **being** a natural horseman, only **aided** and **abetted** Jack in his wild progress.

 **Noun**

A **NOUN** is a word that names a (1.) **person**, (2.) **place**, (3.) **thing**, or (4.) **idea**.

We use the color **YELLOW** to indicate **NOUNS**, because, like the sun, which is **YELLOW** and gives light, **NOUNS** light up a sentence for us.

Examples of Nouns:

Persons – brother, teacher, uncle, doctor, nurse

Places – West Point, field, country, beach, New York

Things – pen, apple, truck, clouds, puppy, lipstick

Ideas – hope, faith, gratitude, boredom, joy

A **compound noun** uses two or more nouns as one, as follows:

Jim Jones, horseshoe, cupcake, Atilla the Hun, self-help

A **collective noun** names a group, as follows:

flock, class, team, family, herd, audience, gaggle (of geese)

HOW TO SPOT A NOUN:

A **NOUN** is the **NAME** of a person, place, thing, or idea.

1. **Person**: Queen Juliana, Gussie
2. **Place**: Europe, home, seashore
3. **Thing**: cat, mountain, castle
4. **Idea**: love, hope, honor, joy

A **COMPOUND NOUN** is **two or more words** used as a single **NOUN**, as in *Queen Juliana* or *seashore*.

A **COLLECTIVE NOUN** names **a group**, as in family, servants, herd, flock, or team.

A **COMMON NOUN** names **a person, place, thing, or idea**, but does not say which particular one.

A **PROPER NOUN** names **a particular person, place, or thing**, and always begins with a capital letter.

We underline **NOUNS** with yellow because they tell us what the sentence is all about; when we find discover a **NOUN** in a sentence, it is as if the sun has suddenly come out.

NOUNS may appear anywhere in the sentence – beginning, middle, or end. Look for a **NOUN** at the end of a **PREPOSITIONAL PHRASE**. **NOUNS** and **PRONOUNS** are always interchangeable.

FIND THE NOUNS AND MARK THEM IN YELLOW:

Today, if Sergio happens to be away at school when a foxhunt originates at the palace stables, Jack is heard whinnying with rage. He knows he cannot join the hunt unless Sergio is at home. In winter, when the King and Queen are not so busy with state events, the family spends time together after the evening meal. The girls often beg their father to tell the story of how he and their mother met and fell in love. They have heard it many times, but it never fails to delight them.

"Well, we were both at a ski resort in Austria," he begins, "but we had never met. Your mother was from Scandinavia, and this was her first visit to Austria. In the evening the skiers would meet in the lodge for conversation.

I noticed your mother the moment she walked in that evening. She was beautiful in a blue cashmere sweater that matched her eyes, and I couldn't stop looking at her.

(A **piebald** horse is black with large white spots.)

ANSWER KEY:

Today, if **Sergio** happens to be away at **school** when a **foxhunt** originates at the palace **stables**, **Jack** is heard whinnying with **rage**. He knows he cannot join the **hunt** unless **Sergio** is at **home**. In **winter**, when the **King** and **Queen** are not so busy with state **events**, the **family** spends **time** together after the evening **meal**. The **girls** often beg their **father** to tell the **story** of how he and their **mother** met and fell in **love**. They have heard it many **times**, but it never fails to delight them.

"Well, we were both at a ski **resort** in **Austria**," he begins, "but we had never met. Your **mother** was from **Scandinavia**, and this was her first **visit** to **Austria**. In the evening the **skiers** would meet in the **lodge** for **conversation**.

I noticed your **mother** the **moment** she walked in that **evening**. She was beautiful in a blue cashmere **sweater** that matched her **eyes**, and I couldn't stop looking at her.

FIND THE NOUNS AND MARK THEM IN YELLOW:

"Finally everyone drifted off to bed, and fortunately, she lingered. I went over and introduced myself. She said she hadn't seen me before. I told her that I had just arrived. I explained that I couldn't come earlier because of my avuncular duties.

"'And what were those?'" she asked.

"'Actually, I have two nephews. Earlier I had promised to take them to see the Lipizzaner stallions when they were next in our area. Their performance was held yesterday.' I replied."

That was the Queen's cue to break in. "And I knew at once, girls, that this was the man I wanted to marry. Any man who could use the word *avuncular* in everyday conversation was the man for me!"

"And then what happened?" the girls would ask.

"Why, we stayed up and talked until dawn," their father would say.

"We had so much to catch up on, you see," the Queen would add.

ANSWER KEY:

"Finally everyone drifted off to **bed**, and fortunately, she lingered. I went over and introduced myself. She said she hadn't seen me before. I told her that I had just arrived. I explained that I couldn't come earlier because of my avuncular **duties**.

"'And what were those?'" she asked.

"'Actually, I have two **nephews**. Earlier I had promised to take them to see the Lipizzaner **stallions** when they were next in our **area**. Their **performance** was held yesterday.' I replied."

That was the Queen's **cue** to break in. "And I knew at once, **girls**, that this was the **man** I wanted to marry. Any **man** who could use the **word** avuncular in everyday **conversation** was the **man** for me!"

"And then what happened?" the **girls** would ask.

"Why, we stayed up and talked until **dawn**," their **father** would say.

"We had so much to catch up on, you see," the **Queen** would add.

(**Avuncular** means: "kind or friendly like an uncle".)

FIND THE NOUNS AND MARK THEM IN YELLOW:

"That night we started a life-long conversation that has never ended," the King would say.

For a few moments no one would speak. The familiar crackling of the logs in the fireplace was the only sound. The girls were both thinking of their own futures: when would they meet their prince, and would they recognize him as quickly as their mother had recognized their father?

Lady Cassandra

The girls have a governess named Lady Cassandra. She does not particularly care for animals. She is, however, young enough to play games with the princesses and to take them on fascinating outings. She has the strange idea that young people should learn Latin, so that is one of the subjects that the girls study every day.

ANSWER KEY:

"That **night** we started a life-long **conversation** that has never ended," the **King** would say.

For a few **moments** no one would speak. The familiar **crackling** of the **logs** in the **fireplace** was the only **sound**. The **girls** were both thinking of their own **futures**: when would they meet their **prince**, and would they recognize him as quickly as their **mother** had recognized their **father**?

Lady Cassandra

The **girls** have a **governess** named **Lady Cassandra**. She does not particularly care for **animals**. She is, however, young enough to play **games** with the **princesses** and to take them on fascinating **outings**. She has the strange **idea** that young **people** should learn **Latin**, so that is **one** of the **subjects** that the **girls** study every **day**.

Pronoun

A PRONOUN is a word that takes the place of a NOUN.

These PRONOUNS act as the subject in a sentence: I, you, he, she, it, we, you, they

These PRONOUNS act as the object in a sentence: me, you, him, her, it, us, them

We use the color ORANGE to indicate PRONOUNS because ORANGE is similar to YELLOW as NOUNS are similar to PRONOUNS.

There are six kinds of pronouns:
1. Personal: (I, me, we, us, my, mine, our, ours, you, your, yours, he, she, it, they, him, her, hers, its, their, theirs) These all refer to a speaker.
2. Interrogative: (who, whom, whose, which, what) These are used to ask a question.
3. Demonstrative: (this, that, these, those) These point out the person or thing being referred to.
4. Indefinite: (each, either, one, anybody, some, more, all) These point out persons or things that are not specifically named.
5. Compound: (myself, ourselves, yourself, yourselves, himself, herself, itself, oneself, themselves) These are combined with self or selves.
6. Relative: (who, whom, whose, which, that) These are used to introduce dependent clauses. (We will explain this later.)

HOW TO SPOT A PRONOUN:

A **PRONOUN** is a word that takes the place of a **NOUN**.

There are six kinds of **PRONOUNS**. They are listed below, with a few examples of each one. Feel free to refer back to this list when searching for **PRONOUNS**.

1. **Personal** pronouns: (These refer to the **speaker**).
    Examples: I, me, we, us, my, mine, our, ours.

2. **Interrogative** pronouns: (These are used to **ask a question**).
    Examples: who, whom, whose, which, what.

3. **Demonstrative** pronouns: (These **point out a noun in the sentence**).
    Examples: this, that, these, those.

4. **Indefinite** pronouns: (These **point out persons or things** that are not specifically named in the sentence).
    Examples: either, each, one, anybody, some, more, all.

5. **Compound** pronouns: (These combine with *self* or *selves*).
    Examples: myself, ourselves, yourself, himself, themselves.

6. **Relative** pronouns: (These introduce another complete thought into the sentence that you are studying).
    Examples: who, whom, whose, which, that

FIND THE PRONOUNS AND MARK THEM IN ORANGE:

The Cousins

The girls have two cousins who come to visit on a regular basis. Their real names are Claire Elizabeth and Alyssa Rachael, but they are called "Claire -Bear" and "Lyssa-Ray" by their cousins. They are nearly the same age as the two princesses. They live just over the mountain from the castle. The four girls often meet in the sunny valley between their two homes. They have many exciting adventures together. They all love one another like sisters.

Mrs. Grimm

Another person that the princesses see on a regular basis is Mrs. Grimm, the head housekeeper. She pops in and out from time to time to make sure everything is in order, but her presence is rarely noticed. The girls can often hear her coming by the clink, clink of her keys, which she wears on a gold chain around her waist. (When the word *her* appears before a noun, that word becomes an adjective. Example: *her keys*.)

ANSWER KEY:

The Cousins

The girls have two cousins **who** come to visit on a regular basis. Their real names are Claire Elizabeth and Alyssa Rachael, but **they** are called "Claire-Bear" and "Lyssa-Ray" by their cousins. **They** are nearly the same age as the two princesses. **They** live just over the mountain from the castle. The four girls often meet in the sunny valley between their two homes. **They** have many exciting adventures together. **They** all love one another like sisters.

Mrs. Grimm

Another person that the princesses see on a regular basis is Mrs. Grimm, the head housekeeper. **She** pops in and out from time to time to make sure **everything** is in order, but her presence is rarely noticed. The girls can often hear **her** coming by the clink, clink of her keys, which **she** wears on a gold chain around her waist.

FIND THE PRONOUNS AND MARK THEM IN ORANGE:

She is known as "The Chatelaine", (a word from the French meaning *chain*, a reference to her keys). One definition of chatelaine is "one who controls a large house."

The Parlor Maids

Of course the girls know all the upstairs parlor maids; they often pop in and out carrying feather dusters or clean laundry. The lively parlor maids are a fine source of information; from them Gussie and Nessa regularly learn what is currently going on in the rest of the palace.

Grammarland

The name of this realm is Grammarland. It is a small principality located at the foot of the Lesser Alps not far from Austria. Every day in Grammarland the sun shines on her many sparkling, snow-capped mountains. There one can wander at will through fragrant forests of dark green hemlock or stop and pick brilliantly colored alpine flowers in the sunny meadows.

ANSWER KEY:

She is known as "The Chatelaine", (a word from the French, meaning *chain*, a reference to her keys). One definition of chatelaine is "one **who** controls a large house."

The Parlor Maids

Of course the girls know all the upstairs parlor maids; **they** often pop in and out carrying feather dusters or clean laundry. The lively parlor maids are a fine source of information; from **them** Gussie and Nessa regularly learn what is currently going on in the rest of the palace.

Grammarland

The name of this realm is Grammarland. **It** is a small principality located at the foot of the Lesser Alps not far from Austria. Every day in Grammarland the sun shines on her many sparkling, snow-capped mountains. There **one** can wander at will through fragrant forests of dark green hemlock or stop and pick brilliantly colored alpine flowers in the sunny meadows.

FIND THE PRONOUNS AND MARK THEM IN ORANGE:

Here birds sing, squirrels scamper, and soft-eyed stags peer through the bushes. Ah, Grammarland. . .

Mrs. BCE Grubb

Mrs. Grubb is the head cook at Greytowers. Her initials stand for the following: **Best Cook Ever**. Gussie and Nessa added these initials to her name some years ago, and she was really rather pleased. It is true that Mrs. Grubb has a wide reputation throughout the kingdom for her delicious meals.

In winter she serves her home made cream of potato soup well seasoned with fresh herbs grown on the sunny windows over the sinks in the palace kitchen; it is thick enough for a spoon to stand upright in the bowl. It really hits the spot. In summer her pink lemonade and crisp raspberry pies are consumed by all at an alarmingly fast rate. Everyone says you haven't really lived until you have tasted her famous cinnamon buns fresh from the oven. These are the best ever!

ANSWER KEY:

Here birds sing, squirrels scamper, and soft-eyed stags peer through the bushes. Ah, Grammarland...

Mrs. BCE Grubb

Mrs. Grubb is the head cook at Greytowers. Her initials stand for the following: **Best Cook Ever**. Gussie and Nessa added these initials to her name some years ago, and **she** was really rather pleased. It is true that Mrs. Grubb has a wide reputation throughout the kingdom for her delicious meals.

In winter **she** serves her home made cream of potato soup well seasoned with fresh herbs grown on the sunny windows over the sinks in the palace kitchen; **it** is thick enough for a spoon to stand upright in the bowl. **It** really hits the spot. In summer her pink lemonade and crisp raspberry pies are consumed by **all** at an alarmingly fast rate. **Everyone** says **you** haven't really lived until **you** have tasted her famous cinnamon buns fresh from the oven. **These** are the best ever!

Adjective

An **ADJECTIVE** is a word that modifies (or describes) a noun or a pronoun. It answers these questions: **what kind? Which one? How many? How much? Or whose?**.

We use the color **RED** to indicate an adjective, because **RED** is a pretty, decorative color, and adjectives decorate sentences as well.

ADJECTIVES tend to cluster around a **NOUN**. Several **ADJECTIVES** may appear around one **NOUN** and describe that **NOUN** in full.

The words *a*, *an*, and *the* are called **ARTICLES**. **ARTICLES** are really **ADJECTIVES**, because they always modify a **NOUN**.

POSSESSIVE NOUNS as in "**Emmeline's** box" and **POSSESSIVE PRONOUNS** as in "**her** box" act as **ADJECTIVES** in a sentence.

HOW TO SPOT AN ADJECTIVE:

An **ADJECTIVE** is a word that **describes (modifies)** a NOUN or PRONOUN.

It answers the following questions: **What kind? Which one? How many? How much? Whose?**

Most **ADJECTIVES** are clustered around the NOUN or PRONOUN that they describe.

Several **ADJECTIVES** may describe the same word.

The words *a*, *an*, and *the* are always **ADJECTIVES**. These pronouns are called *articles*.

NOUNS and PRONOUNS that show **possession** are usually called **ADJECTIVES**. A NOUN that has an **apostrophe** becomes an **ADJECTIVE**.

Examples: Donald's bicycle; his license; Anna's purse; her cat.

Note: In the practice pages on **ADJECTIVES**, I will underline the NOUNS in yellow and the PRONOUNS in orange. Look for words clustered around the yellow NOUNS and orange PRONOUNS.

Mark these words in red. Take time to look back and see how they relate to the NOUNS and PRONOUNS.

FIND THE **ADJECTIVES**. MARK THEM IN **RED**:

She is known throughout the kingdom for her **delicious** **iced** tea, which King Constantine calls "the nectar of the gods."

Her **brown** eyes sparkle with anticipation as she enters the **morning** room promptly at nine to plan out the day's menus with Queen Juliana.

She proudly carries her **spiral** notebook and wears a **freshly starched** **white** apron with ruffles and a **lace-trimmed matching** cap. She has **soft, curly chestnut-brown** hair that she keeps rather short, but she cannot seem to keep a **few recalcitrant** curls from peeping out here and there.

Her cheeks are flushed from rushing around the **warm** kitchen, and her dimples are deep for she is smiling at the thought of planning yet another **culinary** triumph with the **resourceful** Queen.

She does remind one of a **wind-up** toy that is **fully wound**.

ANSWER KEY:

She is known throughout **the** kingdom for **her delicious iced** tea, which King Constantine calls "**the** nectar of **the** gods."

Her brown eyes sparkle with anticipation as she enters **the morning room** promptly at nine to plan out **the day's** menus with Queen Juliana.

She proudly carries **her spiral** notebook and wears **a** freshly **starched white** apron with ruffles and **a lace-trimmed matching** cap. She has **soft, curly chestnut- brown** hair that she keeps rather **short**, but she cannot seem to keep **a few recalcitrant** curls from peeping out here and there.

Her cheeks are **flushed** from rushing around **the warm kitchen**, and **her** dimples are **deep** for she is smiling at **the** thought of planning yet **another culinary** triumph with **the resourceful** Queen.

She does remind one of **a wind-up** toy that is fully **wound**.

FIND THE ADJECTIVES. MARK THEM IN RED:

Uncle Wilmont

Uncle Wilmont is the **head** gardener. He is not anyone's **real** uncle, but ever since Gussie and Nessa were **young** children they called him Uncle Wilmont, and the name has stuck. His **real** name is Mr. Wilmont Billingsley, and he is the **fifth** generation of Billingsleys who have tilled the soil at the palace. His knowledge of vegetables and fruits – which varieties grow best where, when to plant, when to harvest, and how to cultivate and fertilize – cannot be matched by anyone else in the kingdom.

There are **two** things of interest about Uncle Wilmont, at least as far as the girls are concerned. He has a **shiny gold** tooth (it is his **left eye** tooth), that sparkles when he laughs (which is often); and he tells the **best** stories in the world. Every subject one might bring up reminds Uncle Wilmont of a story. He always laughs uproariously at his **own** jokes even if he has told them **six dozen** times. He is a **keen** observer of **human** nature and a **born** storyteller.

ANSWER KEY:

Uncle Wilmont

Uncle Wilmont is **the head gardener.** He is not **anyone's real uncle**, but ever since **Gussie** and **Nessa** were **young children** they called him **Uncle Wilmont**, and **the name** has stuck. **His real name** is **Mr. Wilmont Billingsley**, and he is **the fifth generation** of Billingsleys who have tilled **the soil** at **the palace**. His **knowledge** of **vegetables** and **fruits** – **which varieties** grow best where, when to plant, when to harvest, and how to cultivate and fertilize – cannot be matched by anyone **else** in the **kingdom**.

There are **two things** of **interest** about **Uncle Wilmont**, at least as far as **the girls** are concerned. He has **a shiny gold tooth** (it is his **left eye tooth**), that sparkles when he laughs (which is often); and he tells the **best stories** in **the world**. **Every subject** one might bring up reminds **Uncle Wilmont** of **a story**. He always laughs uproariously at **his own jokes** even if he has told them **six dozen times**. He is **a keen observer** of **human nature** and **a born storyteller**.

FIND THE ADJECTIVES. MARK THEM IN RED:

Most days Uncle Wilmont comes to the morning room after Mrs. Grubb leaves so that he can tell the Queen which fruits and vegetables are at their peak that day. In winter he grows certain fresh foods in his many greenhouses, so there is always something healthy and tasty to suggest for the day's menus. The Queen tells him what fresh produce she wants him to take to Mrs. Grubb and her staff after he has finished his interview with her.

Aunt Hilda

Aunt Hilda is not really the girls' aunt, but their great aunt. She is the sister of King Constantine's mother, and she loves to travel. She has visited more out-of-the-way corners of the globe than one could name, yet she never seems to tire of packing another suitcase and leaving on another extended tour. Between trips she lives in a large and lovely bedroom on the fourth floor of the castle.

The girls look forward to her visits because she often comes to the schoolroom and regales them with amazing stories of her many trips.

ANSWER KEY:

Most days **Uncle Wilmont** comes to **the morning room** after **Mrs. Grubb** leaves so that he can tell **the Queen** which fruits and **vegetables** are at **their peak that day**. In **winter** he grows **certain fresh foods** in **his many greenhouses**, so there is always something **healthy** and **tasty** to suggest for **the day's menus**. **The Queen** tells him what **fresh produce** she wants him to take to **Mrs. Grubb** and **her staff** after he has finished **his interview** with her.

Aunt Hilda

Aunt Hilda is not really **the girls' aunt**, but **their great aunt.** She is the **sister** of **King Constantine's mother**, and she loves to travel. She has visited **more out-of-the-way corners** of **the globe** than one could name, yet she never seems to tire of packing **another suitcase** and leaving on **another extended tour**. Between **trips** she lives in **a large** and **lovely bedroom** on **the fourth floor** of **the castle**.

    The girls look forward to **her visits** because she often comes to **the schoolroom** and regales them with **amazing stories** of her **many trips**.

Adverb

An **ADVERB** is a word that modifies (or describes) a **VERB**, **ADJECTIVE**, or another **ADVERB**. An adverb answers these questions: **where? when? how? how often? how much? to what extent?** (Hint: adverbs very often end in *ly*.)

We use the color **PURPLE** to indicate an adverb, because **PURPLE** is a **KINGLY** color, and the word kingly ends in *ly*.

Examples: hid **there** (**where**?) left **later** (**when**?) walked **softly** (**how**?) **usually** wins (**how often**?) **fully** understood (**to what extent**?)

The word ***not*** or its contraction, ***n't***, is a frequently used **ADVERB**.

Example: did **not** stay, was**n't** asked

ADVERBS describe **VERBS** most of the time, and they usually appear before or after the **VERB**; however, they also describe **ADJECTIVES** or another **ADVERB**.

HOW TO SPOT AN ADVERB:

An **ADVERB** is a word that describes (modifies) a **VERB**, an **ADJECTIVE**, or another **ADVERB**. We use the color **purple** to denote the idea that an **ADVERB** is a **kingly** part of speech.

Many **ADVERBS** end in *ly*, making the memory hook *kingly* – with its *ly* ending – relevant. Furthermore, since the **ADVERB** modifies **three** parts of speech, it surely has a **kingly** position among the parts of speech.

The first thing to remember in seeking to spot an **ADVERB** is this: Which of these five questions does the **ADVERB** answer? All **ADVERBS** answer one of the following questions:

Where? When? How? How often? To what extent?

Examples: *hid there* (**where**); *left later* (**when**); *spoke softly* (**how**); *usually wins* (**how often**); *fully agreed* (**to what extent**).

The word **not** or its contraction **n't** is a frequently used **ADVERB**.

Examples: *did not leave*; *wasn't told*; *hadn't heard*; *would not go*.

Most **ADVERBS** cluster around **VERBS**.

FIND THE ADVERBS AND MARK THEM IN PURPLE:

Their governess, Lady Cassandra, who faithfully teaches the girls English, Latin, and history, loves to invite her into the schoolroom to deeply inform them about the history and geography of the land of her very latest adventures.

Perhaps you will remember that Gussie and Nessa's two cousins, Claire-Bear and Lyssa-Ray, live just over the next mountain. These girls are carefully driven to the palace every day in an ancient Rolls Royce by an equally ancient chauffeur for their lessons. The four girls greatly enjoy studying together and Lady Cassandra says she truly enjoys having four students rather than just two.

The four girls constantly update a large map of the world that hangs on the schoolroom wall, patiently keeping it current with Aunt Hilda's trips by using brightly-colored stickpins to mark out her routes. All the girls wonder what she will do when she sadly runs out of places to visit. "You will run out of stickpins first," she coyly says with a bright smile.

ANSWER KEY:

Their governess, Lady Cassandra, who **faithfully** teaches the girls English, Latin, and history, loves to invite her into the schoolroom to **deeply** inform them about the history and geography of the land of her **very** latest adventures.

Perhaps you will remember that Gussie and Nessa's two cousins, Claire-Bear and Lyssa-Ray, live **just** over the next mountain. These girls are **carefully** driven to the palace every day in an ancient Rolls Royce by an **equally** ancient chauffeur for their lessons. The four girls **greatly** enjoy studying **together** and Lady Cassandra says she **truly** enjoys having four students rather than just two.

The four girls **constantly** update a large map of the world that hangs on the schoolroom wall, **patiently** keeping it current with Aunt Hilda's trips by using **brightly**-colored stickpins to mark out her routes. All the girls wonder what she will do when she **sadly** runs out of places to visit. "You will run out of stickpins first," she **coyly** says with a bright smile.

FIND THE ADVERBS. MARK THEM IN PURPLE:

The word for Aunt Hilda is *flamboyant*. She often appears in her favorite dress of bright turquoise with silver and white lace on its many ruffles.

Thanks to her hairdresser, in spite of her rather advanced age, she is fortunately still a brunette with shoulder-length, wavy tresses. She often likes to pin a fresh rose, preferably red, over her left ear, a quirky habit she picked up on a previous visit to Hawaii. The girls truly love their seemingly ageless Aunt Hilda.

Mrs. Beasley

Mrs. Beasley can truly be described as "mostly brown". She is the girls' science and mathematics teacher. She is a matter-of-fact sort of person, one who deeply loves the symmetry of numbers and the regular rhythms of nature. She likes repetition. The girls always like to keep count of how many brown dresses, jumpers, skirts, and sweaters she owns. These come in many hues, but they are all some shade of "mostly brown".

ANSWER KEY:

The word for Aunt Hilda is *flamboyant*. She **often** appears in her favorite dress of **bright** turquoise with silver and white lace on its many ruffles.

Thanks to her hairdresser, in spite of her **rather** advanced age, she is **fortunately** still a brunette with shoulder-length, wavy tresses. She **often** likes to pin a fresh rose, **preferably** red, over her left ear, a **quirky** habit she picked up on a previous visit to Hawaii. The girls **truly** love their **seemingly** ageless Aunt Hilda.

Mrs. Beasley

Mrs. Beasley can **truly** be described as "**mostly** brown". She is the girls' science and mathematics teacher. She is a matter-of-fact sort of person, one who **deeply** loves the symmetry of numbers and the regular rhythms of nature. She likes repetition. The girls **always** like to keep count of how many brown dresses, jumpers, skirts, and sweaters she owns. These come in many hues, but they are all some shade of "**mostly** brown".

FIND THE ADVERBS. MARK THEM IN PURPLE:

At Christmas one year, the girls bought her a sparkling cameo brooch which she faithfully wears as often as possible. The girls truly think it constantly reflects the sparkle of her quiet sense of humor.

The girls often ask her a question that they think is definitely unanswerable, and she always comes up with a very clever answer on the spur of the moment. Her humor is softly gentle, like her quiet personality.

Here are some examples of her very ready wit:

"Mrs. Beasley," Nessa says, "where was the Great Charter of Grammarland signed?"

"At the very bottom, Dear," answers Mrs. Beasley quickly.

"Mrs. Beasley," says Lissa-Ray, "What happened in 1492?"

"1491 surely ended, My Dear," Mrs. Beasley softly replies.

ANSWER KEY:

At Christmas one year, the girls bought her a sparkling cameo brooch which she **faithfully** wears as **often** as possible. The girls **truly** think it **constantly** reflects the sparkle of her quiet sense of humor.

The girls **often** ask her a question that they think is **definitely** unanswerable, and she **always** comes up with a **very** clever answer on the spur of the moment. Her humor is **softly** gentle, like her quiet personality.

Here are some examples of her **very** ready wit:

"Mrs. Beasley," Nessa says, "where was the Great Charter of Grammarland signed?"

"At the **very** bottom, Dear," answers Mrs. Beasley **quickly**.

"Mrs. Beasley," says Lissa-Ray, "What happened in 1492?"

"1491 **surely** ended, My Dear," Mrs. Beasley **softly** replies.

The King's English

Preposition

A PREPOSITION is a word that shows how a NOUN or PRONOUN is related to some other word in the sentence. A PREPOSITION appears at the beginning of a phrase (a group of related words) and a NOUN or a PRONOUN always appear at the end of the phrase. EXAMPLES of a PREPOSITIONAL PHRASE: "under the bridge", "between the cracks, "over the rainbow", around the corner".

The PREPOSITIONAL PHRASE will be easy to find if you visualize the palace cat Emmeline and her favorite blue box.

Use this sentence: "The cat goes toward the box." Since the phrase "toward the box" starts with a PREPOSITION and ends with a NOUN, you can be sure it is a PREPOSITIONAL PHRASE. Now substitute any of the following PREPOSITIONS for the word "goes" in the above sentence. It will read like this: The cat goes aboard, above, across, after, against, around, at, behind, below, beneath, beside, by, from, in, into, without, near, off on, over, past, to, toward, under or upon the box. Get the picture?

68

HOW TO SPOT A PREPOSITION:

A **PREPOSITION** is a word that shows how a **NOUN** or **PRONOUN** is related to the sentence. Visualize a cat approaching a blue box.

Examples: The cat sat (**on** the box). The cat stood (**beside** the box). The cat climbed (**onto** the box). The cat crawled (**through** the box). The cat hid (**under** the box). The cat jumped (**over** the box).

Notice: the **PREPOSITION always** appears as the first word of a **phrase**. A phrase is **a group of related words**. The related words that I have parenthesized above each make up a **phrase**.

This is important: the **PREPOSITION always** appears in a phrase that **starts** with a **PREPOSITION**, **ends** with a **NOUN**, and often has one or more **ADJECTIVES** in the middle. The **NOUN** at the end of the phrase is called the **object** of the **PREPOSITION**.

In this manual the **PREPOSITIONAL PHRASE** always appears in **parenthesis**. The **PREPOSITION** and its **NOUN** and **ADJECTIVES** are married in that they stay together. We could say that these **parentheses** serve as the wedding ring – proof of their union.

These are exceptions: **but, during, except, since, and until**.

FIND THE PREPOSITIONS. MARK THEM IN BLUE:

The Maestro

We have saved the best *for* last. All four *of* the girls look forward *to* their music lessons because they so much enjoy visits *from* The Maestro.

He does have a regular name, but the two older girls started calling him "The Maestro" when they started taking piano lessons *from* him *at* the ages *of* six and seven, and the name has stuck *with* him.

He comes three days a week *with* his black leather briefcase. He is always just a little late, always slightly breathless, but he is never unprepared. He keeps a fine, full, reddish-brown moustache. He wears a fine gold ring *with* a border *of* diamonds that sparkle when he plays the piano.

He wears a well-tailored corduroy jacket *in* cool weather. He also wears his love *of* music *like* an overcoat, always ready to interrupt himself and share an interesting anecdote *about* some musician.

ANSWER KEY:

The Maestro

We have saved the best (**for** last). All four (**of** the girls) look forward (**to** their music lessons) because they so much enjoy visits (**from** The Maestro).

He does have a regular name, but the two older girls started calling him "The Maestro" when they started taking piano lessons (**from** him) at the ages (**of** six and seven), and the name has stuck (**with** him).

He comes three days a week (**with** his black leather briefcase). He is always just a little late, always slightly breathless, but he is never unprepared. He keeps a fine, full, reddish-brown moustache. He wears a fine gold ring (**with** a border) (**of** diamonds) that sparkle when he plays the piano.

He wears a well-tailored corduroy jacket (**in** cool weather). He also wears his love (**of** music) like an overcoat, always ready to interrupt himself and share an interesting anecdote (**about** some musician).

FIND THE PREPOSITIONS. MARK THEM IN BLUE:

He is very patient with the girls when they are learning a new song. His very attitude makes them want to practice, and – truth be told – all four of them **do** work very hard on their music after classes are over each day.

Sometimes he takes them to matinee concerts. Since he is so thorough, he brings recordings of the music to be played at an upcoming concert for the girls to hear before the event.

He explains what they should listen for. This practice greatly enhances the girls' love, appreciation, and understanding of classical music.

The Morning Room

Queen Juliana has a very comfortable and sunny room on the third floor of the palace that she calls her "morning room". She goes there after breakfast each day, and all the head servants come to confer with her, one by one. At this time she gives orders for the day's work and in turn she receives reports from them.

ANSWER KEY:

He is very patient (**with** the girls) when they are learning a new song. His very attitude makes them want to practice, and – truth be told – all four (**of** them) **do** work very hard (**on** their music) after classes are over (**each** day).

Sometimes he takes them (**to** matinee concerts). Since he is so thorough, he brings recordings (**of** the music) to be played (**at** an upcoming concert) (**for** the girls) to hear (**before** the event).

He explains what they should listen for. This practice greatly enhances the girls' love, appreciation, and understanding (**of** classical music).

The Morning Room

Queen Juliana has a very comfortable and sunny room (**on** the third floor) (**of** the palace) that she calls her "morning room". She goes there (**after** breakfast)(**each** day), and all the head servants come to confer (**with** her), one by one. (**At** this time) she gives orders (**for** the day's work) and (**in** turn) she receives reports (**from** them).

FIND THE PREPOSITIONS. MARK THEM IN BLUE:

The four girls love to spend time **in** the morning room **before** their classes begin. Mrs. Grimm and her staff have arranged a sunny corner **with** a round table and four chairs where they often sit and play scrabble or work a puzzle together. They enjoy honing their Scrabble skills, for they hope to be better competitors when Sergio next comes home **on** holiday.

The girls wait to hear the tinkling **of** Lady Cassandra's bell which calls them to school; **after** all, every governess needs time to prepare her schoolwork **before** her students appear **at** the door each morning.

During this time, Gussie, who is the most ardent **of** the four girls **at** practicing the piano, will pick up her books and say, "Goodbye, Mother; I am going to the classroom to practice my songs."

"**Of** course, Dear; have a nice day," answers the Queen rather absently.

ANSWER KEY:

The four girls love to spend time (**in** the morning room) before their classes begin. Mrs. Grimm and her staff have arranged a sunny corner (**with** a round table and four chairs) where they often sit and play scrabble or work a puzzle together. They enjoy honing their Scrabble skills, for they hope to be better competitors when Sergio next comes home (**on** holiday).

The girls wait to hear the tinkling (**of** Lady Cassandra's bell) which calls them (**to** school); after all, every governess needs time to prepare her schoolwork before her students appear (**at** the door) each morning.

(**During** this time), Gussie, who is the most ardent (**of** the four girls) at practicing the piano, will pick up her books and say, "Goodbye, Mother; I am going (**to** the classroom) to practice my songs."

"Of course, Dear; have a nice day," answers the Queen rather absently.

FIND THE PREPOSITIONS. MARK THEM IN BLUE:

As soon as Gussie enters the classroom she greets Lady Cassandra with a warm smile. Like all students, she is expert at gauging exactly what sort of a mood her teacher is in that day. She notices the expression on her face and listens to the tone of her reply. The two of them discuss the weather while Gussie arranges her music on the piano.

Then she begins to practice. The three girls in the morning room listen intently, but they continue doing whatever is at hand. If she plays a slow dirge or perhaps a hymn like "Abide with me; fast falls the evening tide. . ." the girls know that Lady Cassandra is not in the lightest of moods that day. However, if she swings into a section of "The Beautiful Blue Danube", playing it with particular verve and spirit, the girls will share a secret smile around the table, knowing that Lady Cassandra will be her normal happy self as they go trooping into the schoolroom.

Ah, the language of childhood. . .

ANSWER KEY:

As soon as Gussie enters the classroom she greets Lady Cassandra (**with** a warm smile). Like all students, she is expert at gauging exactly what sort of a mood her teacher is in that day. She notices the expression (**on** her face) and listens to the tone (**of** her reply). The two them discuss the weather while Gussie arranges her music (**on** the piano).

Then she begins to practice. The three girls (**in** the morning room) listen intently, but they continue doing whatever is (**at** hand). If she plays a slow dirge or perhaps a hymn like "Abide with me; fast falls the evening tide. . ." the girls know that Lady Cassandra is not in the lightest (**of** moods) that day. However, if she swings (**into** a section) (**of** "The Beautiful Blue Danube"), playing it (**with** particular verve and spirit), the girls will share a secret smile (**around** the table), knowing that Lady Cassandra will be her normal happy self as they go trooping (**into** the schoolroom).

Ah, the language of childhood. . .

Conjunction

A **CONJUNCTION** is a word that joins words or groups of words. Memorize these basic conjunctions: **and, but, or, nor, for, yet**. We use the color **BROWN** to indicate a conjunction because **BROWN** is the color of rope, and rope ties things together, just as conjunctions do.

Here are some more **coordinating CONJUNCTIONS**. Recognize these: **either. . .or, neither. . .nor, both. . .and, not only. . .but also**. These groups of two **CONJUCTIONS** correlate (or connect) two basic ideas in a sentence.

Example: **Neither** Emmeline **nor** Gussie would ever eat dog food.

Many times **subordinating CONJUNCTIONS** are used to introduce a part of the sentence that explains the main VERB. Recognize these: **as, at, as soon as, after, although, because, before, since, so that, then, unless, until, when, whenever, where, wherever, while**.

Example: **Although** Emmeline was hungry, she refused to eat dog food.

HOW TO SPOT A CONJUNCTION:

A **CONJUCTION** is a word that joins words or groups of words.

The seven most famous **COORDINATING CONJUNCTIONS** can be learned by remembering the acronym **FANBOYS**:

<u>F</u>or – <u>A</u>nd – <u>N</u>or – <u>B</u>ut – <u>O</u>r – <u>Y</u>et – <u>S</u>o.

The Merrian-Webster dictionary defines *fanboys* as follows: a boy or man who is an extremely or overly enthusiastic fan of someone or something.

Memorize these **CONJUNCTIONS** that appear in pairs:
either – or; neither – nor; both – and; not only – but also.

Study this long list of **CONJUNCTIONS**. They are used to introduce a **dependent clause** into a sentence:

after, although, as, as if, as much as, as long as, as soon as, because, before, if, in order that, since, so that, than, though, unless, until, when, whenever, where, wherever, while.

We use the color **brown** to identify the **CONJUNCTION** because **brown** reminds us of rope. Rope ties any number of **things** together, and **CONJUNCTIONS** tie any number of **words** as well as any number of **sentence parts** together. Where would we be without **CONJUNCTIONS**?

FIND THE CONJUNCTIONS AND MARK THEM IN BROWN:

1. Emmeline is the Queen's cat, and Marceline belongs to Gussie.
2. Although both cats live at Greytowers, each has her own room.
3. Because Emmeline is the Queen's cat, she believes that she takes priority over Marceline and Smokey.
4. Neither Marceline nor Smokey like this idea.
5. Not only does Emmeline boss the other cats, but she also tries to boss Queen Juliana well as the princesses.
6. Whenever King Constantine comes into the room, Emmeline jumps on the sofa and Marceline vanishes.
7. Neither Emmeline nor Marceline enjoy being brushed and combed.
8. Since Smokey has short hair, he enjoys being groomed.
9. Although everyone calls him "Smokey", he also answers to "Smoking Gun", as this was the name his owner gave him.
10. Since Smokey is a cat, he trusts in his sharp claws and teeth.
11. Because he is a natural hunter, all the palace mice scatter when he struts down the hallway.
12. Since the palace is so spacious, the cats often get lost.

ANSWER KEY:

1. Emmeline is the Queen's cat, **and** Marceline belongs to Gussie.
2. **Although** both cats live at Greytowers, each has her own room.
3. **Because** Emmeline is the Queen's cat, she believes that she takes priority over Marceline **and** Smokey.
4. **Neither** Marceline **nor** Smokey like this idea.
5. **Not only** does Emmeline boss the other cats, **but** she **also** tries to boss Queen Juliana **as well as** the princesses.
6. **Whenever** King Constantine comes into the room, Emmeline jumps on the sofa **and** Marceline vanishes.
7. **Neither** Emmeline **nor** Marceline enjoy being brushed **and** combed.
8. **Since** Smokey has short hair, he enjoys being groomed.
9. **Although** everyone calls him "Smokey", he **also** answers to "Smoking Gun", **as** this was the name his owner gave him.
10. **Since** Smokey is a cat, he trusts in his sharp claws **and** teeth.
11. **Because** he is a natural hunter, all the palace mice scatter when he struts down the hallway.
12. **Since** the palace is so spacious, the cats often get lost.

Interjection

An **INTERJECTION** is an exclamatory word that stands alone but is connected to a sentence. It gives the sentence **POWER** and **PUNCH**. Often the interjection expresses strong feeling. Then an exclamation point is used.

We use the color **BLACK** to indicate an **INTERJECTION** because **BLACK** is a strong color and can stand alone just as an **INTERJECTION** does.

Examples of few **INTERJECTIONS**:

BOO! BWAH-HAH-HAH! DUH! EEK! HAH! HEY!

HEE HEE! HO HUM! OUCH! OY, OY, OY! PSST!

WHOOP-DE-DO! YIKES!   YUM! ZOINKS! ZOWIE!

HOW TO SPOT AN INTERJECTION

An **interjection** is a word that expresses strong feeling but is not necessary to the meaning of the sentence. In diagramming we place the **interjection** on its own line next to the sentence.

Below are several sentences that use an **interjection** to add

POWER and **PUNCH** to the statement:

Whoa! You're going too fast around that corner, Daisy!

Boo! I made you jump!

Yikes! There is a thousand-legger in my bedroom!

Ho Hum! I am going to take a nap on the sofa.

Whew! Weeding that flower bed was hard work!

Wow! I didn't expect our team to win today!

Psst! Loan me a pencil, will you?

RELATING THE PARTS OF THE SENTENCE TO ROYALTY:

The VERB is the KING (He is the most important person in the kingdom, just as the verb is the most important word in the sentence)

The SUBJECT is the QUEEN (She is the second most important person in the kingdom, as the subject is the second word we look for when parsing a sentence.)

The COMPLEMENT is the PRINCESS
(The princess completes the family circle, just as the complement completes the thought that goes on the base line.)

ADJECTIVES, ADVERBS, and PREPOSITIONAL PHRASES are the *PALACE WORKERS*.
(The palace workers are essential to the running of the palace, just as the prepositional phrases, adjectives, and adverbs are essential to the rounding out of the sentence. They are not just nice to have, but they are necessary to the full meaning of the statement.)

HOW TO MAKE FRIENDS WITH FLASHCARDS:

There is no substitute for review and repetition. Learn a few basic facts about each part of speech, and you will find that you truly understand the complete concept. I want to help you along this path by suggesting the use of flashcards.

On one side of your 3x5 cards copy the word or words that appear in color. On the other side write the words that appear in black. Take these cards with you – in your pocket or in your purse – and pull them out to review whenever you have a few spare minutes.

1. NOUN (FRONT OF FLASHCARD)
The name of a person, place, thing, or idea (BACK OF FLASHCARD)

2. PRONOUN (FRONT OF FLASHCARD)
Takes the place of a noun. I, you, he, she, it, we, you, they, me, you, him, her, it, us, you, them. (BACK OF FLASHCARD)

3. VERB (FRONT OF FLASHCARD)
Linking: am, is, are, was, were, be, being, been
Action: Ask yourself while looking at the word, "Can I do this thing?"
Intransitive: Shows existence; needs no other word to complete its meaning. (BACK OF FLASHCARD)

4. ADVERB (FRONT OF FLASHCARD)

Describes a verb, adjective, or another adverb. Answers these questions: What kind? Which one? How many? How much? Whose? (BACK OF FLASHCARD)

5. ADJECTIVE (FRONT OF FLASHCARD)

Describes (modifies, or changes) a noun or a pronoun.

Answers these questions: What kind? Which one? How many? How much? Whose? (BACK OF FLASHCARD)

6. PREPOSITION (FRONT OF FLASHCARD)

Always appears at the beginning of a_phrase. (A phrase is a group of related words.) This phrase starts with a preposition and ends with a noun.

EXAMPLE: "I'm sitting (on top) (of the world) (with a rainbow) (on my shoulder)."

A preposition expresses motion, as a cat moves toward a box. It can move around, across, against, behind; below, beside, toward, within; over, under, past, against; to, from, in, or out. (BACK OF FLASHCARD)

7. CONJUNCTION (FRONT OF FLASHCARD)

Connects words and phrases and clauses in a sentence. Memorize the following:

For And Nor But Or Yet So – FANBOYS.

Also remember these conjunctions: although, because, since, unless, whenever, wherever, and while. (BACK OF FLASHCARD)

8. INTERJECTION (FRONT OF FLASHCARD)

An extra word that provides POWER and PUNCH. It stands alone in the sentence, and is usually set off by an exclamation point. (BACK OF FLASHCARD)

How to Parse

"Trumpeter Swan in Flight" by Larry Kitchen

TO PARSE OR NOT TO PARSE: THAT IS THE QUESTION

The word *parse* comes to us directly from the Latin, and it means **"to divide something up into many parts."** In fact, our word for the common herb *parsley* comes directly from the word *parse*. And a sprig of parsley, as you know, is divided into many small parts.

In this instance, we plan to take an **English sentence** apart, dividing it up into its many usages. In order to do this, I plan to teach you a simple **memory hook**. This memory hook is based on the words **FLIP FLOP**. Hereafter, when you see a picture of a pair of **flip flops**, your memory should take you through the **four basic steps of parsing**.

Below is a painting of **Mnemosyne**, ancient Greek goddess of memory, created by the Victorian artist Dante Gabriel Rossetti:

INTERESTING FACTS ABOUT MEMORY:

What is the origin of the word <u>memory</u>? It is based on the name of the Greek goddess of memory, Mnemosyne. Here is how her name is pronounced: neh-**moss**-ah-nee. Notice that the first M is silent.

In English we speak of a **mnemonic tool** or device or system used as an aid to remembering. We often use **acronyms** for this purpose. An **acronym** is a word formed from the initial letters of a name (as in <u>**WAC**</u>, the **W**omen's **A**ir **C**orps. It is also used as a word formed by parts of several words, as in the acronym <u>**RADAR**</u> for **Ra**dio **D**etection **a**nd **R**anging. Both **acronyms** were developed during World War II.

A popular mnemonic device (or **memory hook**) is the **acronym** for remembering the colors of the rainbow. Take the name **Roy G. Biv**: **R**-**r**ed, **O**-**o**range, **Y**-**y**ellow, **G**-**g**reen, **B**-**b**lue, **I**-**i**ndigo, and **V**-**v**iolet.

Memory begins to work twenty weeks after conception. Memory has two components – short term and long term. This is why one can knit and talk on the phone at the same time.

Adults can remember up to one hundred thousand words. However, there is a reason why phone numbers are only seven digits – it is because seven is the maximum capacity for short term memory.

We will use two *memory hooks* to learn how to parse. The first is Flip Flops (FL/FL), and the second is "Hello, I'm OLIVIA".

FLIP FLOPS = FL/FL

1. **FIND** the Verb and its helpers.
2. **LOCATE** the Subject.
3. **FINISH** the Thought (the Complement.)
4. **LOSE** the Prepositional Phrases.

Find, **L**ocate, **F**inish, and **L**ose. Then. . .

1. Mark the Verb in **GREEN** or underline the <u>verb</u> twice.
2. Underline the <u>Subject</u>.
3. Bracket the [Complement].
4. Parenthesize the (Prepositional Phrases).

How to Label a Sentence:

We start with this memory hook: FL/FL (or FLIP/FLOP).

We use the following four steps based on the acronym FL/FL:

1. Find the verb and its helpers.

Please note: The verb and its helpers make up a verb phrase – a group of connected words.

EXAMPLE SENTENCE:

Hope is the heartbeat of the soul.

(In this sentence we see only <u>one small verb</u>, the linking verb <u>is</u>. Underline that with your green marker.)

ANSWER KEY: Hope *is* the heartbeat of the soul.

2. Locate the subject.

Please note: The subject is usually found at the beginning of the sentence. The subject will always be a noun or a pronoun.

Sometimes the subject is an understood pronoun; then you will place an (x) where the subject should be located.

EXAMPLE SENTENCE:

Hope is the heartbeat of the soul.

(In this sentence we see that the subject is the word *hope*; underline it once.)

ANSWER KEY: Hope is the heartbeat of the soul.

3. Finish the thought.

Please note: The complement is the word or words that complete the thought. (In this sentence we see that the object is the word *heartbeat*; bracket it.)

EXAMPLE SENTENCE:

Hope is the heartbeat of the soul.

ANSWER KEY:

Hope is the [heartbeat] of the soul.

4. Lose the Prepositional Phrases.

(In this sentence we see that the prepositional phrase is "of the soul"; parenthesize it.)

Hope is the heartbeat of the soul.

ANSWER KEY:

Hope is the heartbeat (of the soul).

CONGRATULATIONS; YOU ARE NOW ABLE TO LABEL!

A FEW LAST WORDS ABOUT COMPLEMENTS:
A COMPLEMENT COULD APPEAR IN A SENTENCE AS. . .

1. . .a *direct object* (DO) following an action verb (AV).

2. . .a *predicate* noun (PN) or *predicate* adjective (PA) following a linking verb (LV).

3. . .an *objective complement* noun (OC [N]) or an *objective complement* adjective (OC [A]). These are the direct objects of an action verb (AV).

4. . .an *indirect object* of an action verb (IO).

QUESTION: WHEN IS A COMPLIMENT NOT A COMPLIMENT?

ANSWER: WHEN IT IS A COMPLEMENT!

Yes, it's true –we all love compliments. "I like your new hairstyle." "I enjoyed your speech today." "You played a great basketball game." All these compliments are music to our ears.

There is, however, another type of **compliment** – one spelled with an *e* in the middle rather than with an *i*. The **complement** plays an important part in the English sentence. Without the **complement** most of our **sentences** would not make **sense**!

Let's start at the very beginning: First, we will draw a baseline, like this:

__(SUBJECT) | _____(PREDICATE)_____

This baseline represents **the basic thought** that you wish to convey. This thought is divided up between the **subject** and the **predicate**. You already know what the **subject** is, but what is the **predicate**?

The word *predicate* comes from the Latin word *praedicat*. The modern meaning is this: "to affirm, **proclaim**, or assert".

What the **predicate** does is to **proclaim the full meaning** of your sentence.

Your next question should be this: **"What is included in the predicate?"**

The **predicate** always begins (and sometimes ends) with the **verb**. In fact, there are many times when the **predicate** appears as one word.

Here are some EXAMPLES:
The lion | **roared**.
The canoe | **flipped**.
The dog | **barked**.

This **VERB** is a **VERB** that **needs no other word to complete its meaning**. It is called an **INTRANSITIVE VERB**. An **INTRANSITIVE VERB** does not need further explanation. Look at the three examples above. You fully understand those sentences, do you not? So when you see an **INTRANSITIVE VERB** you will know that the **VERB ITSELF** completes the **predicate**.

HOWEVER, OFTEN THE VERB NEEDS A WORD OR TWO TO COMPLETE ITS BASIC MEANING, AND THAT'S WHERE THE COMPLEMENT COMES IN.

THE DIRECT OBJECT

The most common **complement** is the **DIRECT OBJECT**.

                S   AV   DO
EXAMPLE: Mrs. Grubb *stirred* the soup.

NOTICE: The total meaning of the sentence "Mrs. Grubb stirred the soup" would change if we left out the **complement**. Then the sentence would read, "Mrs. Grubb *stirred*." Then it might mean that she turned over in her bed. Then the VERB would be an INTRANSITIVE VERB, which is known as a VERB INTRANSITIVE.

NOTICE: the verb *stirred* is now an ACTION VERB (AV), not a VERB INTRANSITIVE (VI).

RULES FOR THE DIRECT OBJECT:

1. It will always follow an ACTION VERB.
2. It will always be a NOUN or a PRONOUN.

EXAMPLE FOR A **NOUN**: <u>Sergio</u> **ate** the [soup]. (**DO** - **NOUN**)
EXAMPLE FOR A **PRONOUN**: <u>Sergio</u> **ate** [it]. (**DO** -**PRONOUN**)

THE PREDICATE NOUN AND THE PREDICATE ADJECTIVE:

Another common **COMPLEMENT** is the **PREDICATE NOUN** or the **PREDICATE ADJECTIVE**.

The **PREDICATE NOUN** and the **PREDICATE ADJECTIVE** always follow a **LINKING VERB**. A **LINKING VERB** does just what its name suggests: it **LINKS** the **subject** to the **object** of the sentence.

A **Predicate Noun COMPLETES** and **RENAMES** the subject.
EXAMPLE using a **Predicate Noun**:

      S   **LV**   **PN**
<u>Lady Cassandra</u> **is** the [governess].

RULES FOR THE PREDICATE NOUN:

1. It **always** follows a **LINKING VERB**.
2. It **completes** and renames the subject.

EXAMPLE using a **PREDICATE ADJECTIVE**:

       S   **LV**   **PA**

<u>Lady Cassandra</u> **is** [intelligent].

RULES FOR THE PREDICATE ADJECTIVE:

1. It always follows a **LINKING VERB**.
2. It **completes** and **describes** the subject.

Here is a test to help you discover whether the **complement** is a **PREDICATE NOUN** **(PN)** or a **PREDICATE ADJECTIVE** **(PA)**:

Look at this sentence: *The royal robe is purple.* Can you place the **complement** (purple) before the **subject** (robe) in your mind and find that it makes sense? Yes; you can say *purple robe*. Now the **complement** is an **ADJECTIVE** because it **describes** the subject.

Look at this sentence: *The Alps are majestic mountains.* Can you place the **complement** (mountains) before the **subject** (Alps) and find that it makes sense?

No, "Mountains Alps" doesn't make much sense. So the complement is a **NOUN** because it **renames** the subject.

THE SEVEN TYPES OF SENTENCES IN COLOR:

1. Sleepy **dreams** in bed.

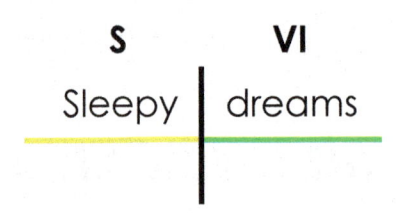

```
     S      VI
  Sleepy | dreams
```

2. Sneezy **found** his handkerchief.

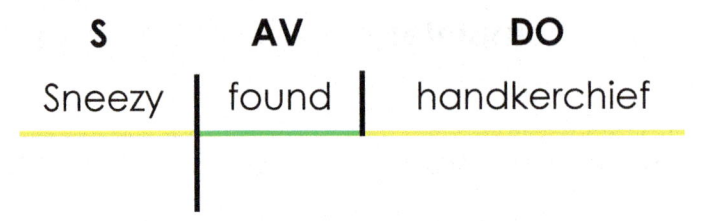

```
     S       AV        DO
  Sneezy | found | handkerchief
```

3. Happy **is** the third dwarf

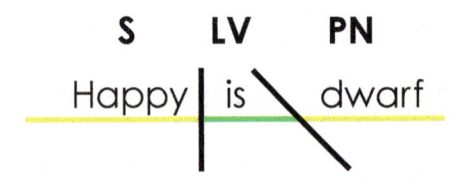

```
    S    LV    PN
  Happy | is \ dwarf
```

4. Doc **is** very intelligent.

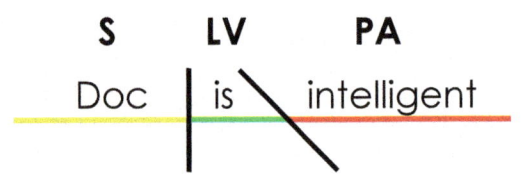

```
    S   LV    PA
   Doc | is \ intelligent
```

5. Grumpy **gave** Snow White a mean look.

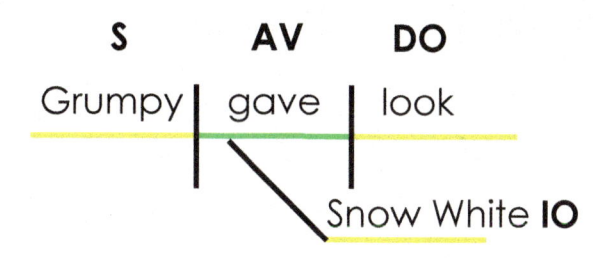

```
           S      AV     DO
        Grumpy | gave | look
        _____|_____|_____
               |
               \ Snow White **IO**
                _____
```

6. Dopey **called** Snow White "Mother"

```
         S        AV        DO           OC-N
       Dopey |  called  | Snow White \  "Mother"
       _____|_____|_____
             |          |
```

7. Bashful **painted** his lunchbox yellow.

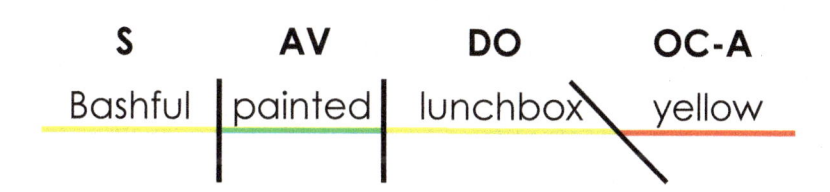

```
         S        AV        DO           OC-A
       Bashful | painted | lunchbox \   yellow
       _____|_____|_____
               |         |
```

The story of *Snow White and the Seven Dwarfs* goes back to antiquity. It is one of the most famous **sevens** of all time. Please become familiar with this important **seven** as well, for it tells you all you need to know about the construction of the basic English sentence.

HOW TO REMEMBER THE THREE TYPES OF VERBS:

OKAY, LET'S GO...
LINKING VERB
VI VERB INTRANSITIVE
ACTION VERB

MEMORY HOOK: OLIVIA

NOW THAT YOU KNOW ALL YOU NEED TO KNOW ABOUT LABELING, LET'S SEE YOU TRY YOUR HAND AT PARSING THE FOLLOWING SENTENCES:

Remember to start with the FL/FL memory hook. Find the verb and mark it in green (or underline it twice). Locate the subject and underline it. Finish the thought and bracket the complement. Finally, Lose the prepositional phrase (or phrases) and parenthesize them.

<u>Fears</u> are paper [tigers].

Good teaching is one-fourth preparation and three fourths theatre.

The summit of Mount Everest is marine limestone.

I awoke with devout thanksgiving for my friends.

Play is really the work of childhood. (Mr. Rogers)

Common sense is not so common. (Voltaire)

(x) Be great in little things. Note: (x) is the understood *you*.

A merry companion is music on a journey.

ANSWER KEY:

<u>Fears</u> **are** paper [tigers].

Good <u>teaching</u> **is** one-fourth [preparation] and three fourths [theatre].

The <u>summit</u> (of Mt. Everest) **is** marine [limestone].

<u>I</u> **awoke** (with devout thanksgiving) (for my friends).

<u>Play</u> **is** really the [work] (of childhood).

Common <u>sense</u> **is** not so [common].

<u>(x)</u> **Be** [great] (in little things).

A merry <u>companion</u> **is** [music] (on a journey).

PARSE THE FOLLOWING SENTENCES:

<u>We</u> **are** [responsible] (to people), not (for them).

Facts are stubborn things.

Hardships often prepare ordinary people for an extraordinary destiny.

Some gifts are big; others are small.

Gifts from the heart are the best gifts of all.

A kind heart is a fountain of gladness.

Great love and great achievements involve great risk.

Yesterday is history.

Tomorrow is mystery.

Today is a gift.

ANSWER KEY:

We **are** [responsible] (to people), not (for them).

Facts **are** stubborn [things].

Hardships often **prepare** ordinary [people] (for an extraordinary destiny).

Some gifts **are** [big], others **are** [small].

Gifts (from the heart) **are** the best [gifts] (of all).

A kind heart **is** a [fountain] (of gladness).

Great love and great achievements **involve** great [risk].

Yesterday **is** [history].

Tomorrow **is** [mystery].

Today **is** a [gift].

THE SEVEN TYPES OF SENTENCES:

          S   VI

1. <u>Gussie</u> **searched**. (**VERB INTRANSITIVE**)

      S   AV   DO

2. <u>Gussie</u> **found** [Marceline]. (**ACTION VERB**)

      S   LV   PN

3. <u>Marceline</u> **is** Gussie's [cat] (**LINKING VERB**)

      S   LV   PA

4. <u>Gussie</u> **was** [clever]. (**LINKING VERB**)

S   AV   IO   DO

5. <u>Gussie</u> **gave** {Marceline} a big [hug]. (**ACTION VERB**)

  S   AV   DO   OC (N)

6. <u>Queen Juliana</u> **named** [Gussie] {"The Feline Detective"}. (**ACTION VERB**)

S   AV   DO OC (A)

7. <u>Gussie</u> **painted Marceline's** favorite [box] {blue}. (**ACTION VERB**)

ABBREVIATIONS USED IN PARSING:

S - Subject   DO - Direct Object   IO - Indirect Object

A - Action Verb   PP - Prepositional Phrase

LV - Linking Verb   OC (A) - Objective Complement (Adjective)

VI - Intransitive Verb   OC (N) - Objective Complement (Noun)

ARE YOU ABLE TO LABEL?

To parse a sentence means to take it apart word by word. Before we can begin to diagram, we must be able to label each part of the sentence. Using the memory hook **FL**/**FL**, let's begin.

1. **F**IND THE VERB:

Since the **VERB** is **KING** in the sentence, we will begin by looking for the **VERB**. First, look for one of the **LINKING VERBS** (**am, is, are, was, were, be, being, been**). If you don't see a **LINKING VERB**, then ask yourself this question: can I **do** this?

Look at the following sentence. What is the thing that you can **do** in that sentence? That's right; you can hold something. You have found your verb. Now mark it in green **or** underline it twice:

The pitcher held the ball in the palm of his hand.
ANSWER KEY: The pitcher held the ball in the palm of his hand.

2. **L**OCATE THE SUBJECT:

The subject will tell you something about the verb. Who held the ball? Yes, it is the pitcher. Underline the subject.

The pitcher held the ball in the palm of his hand.
ANSWER KEY: The <u>pitcher</u> held the ball in the palm of his hand.

3. FIND THE COMPLEMENT:

Look for a word beyond the verb that completes the thought. If you do not need a word to complete the thought, then you may mark the verb as Intransitive (**VI**).

If the verb is a linking verb, mark it this way: Linking Verb (**LV**). Then you will find a **Predicate** that completes the thought. It will be a Predicate NOUN (**renaming** the subject) or a Predicate ADJECTIVE (**describing** the subject).

Since this is not a LINKING VERB, let's go on to the third and final option.

The VERB *held* is an ACTION VERB, for *to hold* is something that you can **do**. So the complement will be a Direct Object (**DO**). Find the Direct Object and bracket it:

> The pitcher held the ball in the palm of his hand.
> **ANSWER KEY:** The <u>pitcher</u> held the [ball] in the palm of his hand.

4. LOCATE THE PREPOSITIONAL PHRASE:

There may be more than one. Parenthesize them.

> The pitcher held the ball in the palm of his hand.
> **ANSWER KEY:** The <u>pitcher</u> held the [ball] (in the palm) (of his hand).

>   S   AV   DO   PP   PP
> The [pitcher] held the [ball] (in the palm) (of his hand).

LABEL THE FOLLOWING SENTENCES:

Wisdom begins in wonder.

No one can help everyone.

Everyone can help someone.

Miracle can grow out of difficulties.

Happiness is the natural flower of goodness.

ANSWER KEY:

     S   VI   PP

Wisdom begins (in wonder).

     S   AV   DO

No one can help [everyone].

     S   AV   DO

Everyone can help [someone].

     S   VI   PP

Miracles can grow out (of difficulties).

     S   LV   DO   PP

Happiness is the natural [flower] (of goodness).

"IT'S ALL ABOUT ME!" -- KING VERB

Although I taught English grammar for twenty-five years, I never noticed until now how all-pervasive is the presence of King Verb! In writing this manual I discovered that it is **impossible to explain any part of speech** without beginning and ending with The King.

When we start to parse and diagram sentences, we cannot proceed until we decide which type of verb we are dealing with -- The King reigns here.

When we start to identify verbals, we soon realize that our language is indeed peppered with words that keep their original use but take on King Verb as their helper.

LONG LIVE KING VERB!

FINDING LINKING VERBS

Now we will find the **LINKING VERB**. Mark it in **green** or underline it twice. Then we will find the subject; underline that once. After that, we will find the Complement (**PREDICATE NOUN**, **PRONOUN**, or **ADJECTIVE**). Bracket that word. Remember, the complement is the word that completes the meaning of the sentence. Finally, if you find a **PREPOSITIONAL PHRASE**, parenthesize it.

Roses are red.

Violets are blue.

No news is good news.

Love is the reason behind everything in this world.

It is well with my soul.

Laughter is inner jogging.

'Be' is a very big two-letter word.

ANSWER KEY:

<u>Roses</u> **are** [red].

<u>Violets</u> **are** [blue].

No <u>news</u> **is** good [news].

<u>Love</u> **is** the [reason] (behind everything) (in this world).

<u>It</u> **is** [well] (with my soul).

<u>Laughter</u> **is** inner [jogging].

<u>'Be'</u> **is** a very big two - letter [word].

FINDING ACTION VERBS

Now we will look for **ACTION VERBS** with understood subjects. In order to show an understood subject, place an **(x)** where the subject should be. Be sure to put parentheses around the **PREPOSITIONAL PHRASES**.

Share your story for Heaven's glory.

Enjoy the little things.

Cast all your cares away.

Delight yourself in your books.

Give thanks for unknown blessings on their way.

Step into the next chapter of your life.

Keep the warmth of the sun in your heart.

ANSWER KEY:

(x) **Share** your [story] (for Heaven's glory).

(x) **Enjoy** the little [things].

(x) **Cast** all your [cares] away.

(x) **Delight** [yourself] (in your books).

(x) **Give** [thanks] (for unknown blessing) (on their way).

(x) **Step** (into the next chapter) (of your life).

(x) **Keep** the [warmth] (of the sun) (in your heart).

FINDING INTRANSITIVE VERBS

Now we look for **INTRANSITIVE VERBS**. Remember that these are **VERBS** that have no object. Later, when you diagram a sentence with an **INTRANSITIVE VERB**, you will place only **two words** on the line, a **subject** and a **verb**. Don't forget to put parenthesis around the prepositional phrases.

Winter is in my head.

Spring is in my heart.

The creation of a thousand forests is in one acorn.

Go with the flow.

Gaze at the sunshine and glance at the problems.

Good judgment comes from experience.

Experience comes from bad judgment.

Good days begin with praise.

ANSWER KEY:

Winter **is** (in my head).

Spring **is** (in my heart).

The creation (of a thousand forests) **is** (in one acorn).

(x) **Go** (with the flow).

(x) **Gaze** (at the sunshine) and **glance** (at the problems).

Good judgment **comes** (from experience).

Experience **comes** (from bad judgment).

Good days **begin** (with praise).

ADD TO YOUR FLASHCARDS:

Remember, there is no substitute for review and repetition. If you will learn the few basic facts listed below, you will truly understand how to parse the basic English sentence.

On one side of your 3x5 cards copy the word or words that appear in color. On the other side, write the words that appear in black. Keep these cards in a convenient spot, then pull them out and review when you have a free moment.

1. ABBREVIATIONS USED IN PARSING: (WRITE THIS TITLE ON THE FRONT)
WRITE THIS INFORMATION ON THE BACK:

S - Subject; DO - Direct Object; IO - Indirect Object; A - Action Verb; PP - Prepositional Phrase; LV - Linking Verb; VI - Verb Intransitive; OC (A) - Objective Complement (Adjective); OC (N) - Objective Complement (Noun).

2. SEVEN TYPES OF SENTENCES: (WRITE THIS TITLE ON THE FRONT)
WRITE THIS INFORMATION ON THE BACK:

(1). Subject + Verb Intransitive; (2). Subject + Action Verb + Direct Object;(3). Subject + Linking Verb + Predicate Noun; (4). Subject + Linking Verb + Predicate Adjective; (5). Subject + Action Verb + Indirect

Object + Direct Object; (6). Subject + Action Verb + Direct Object + Objective Complement - Noun; (7). Subject + Action Verb + Direct Object + Objective Complement - Adjective.

MEMORY HOOK FOR PARSING THE BASIC SENTENCE: (WRITE THIS TITLE ON THE FRONT)

WRITE THIS INFORMATION ON THE BACK:

FL/FL = FLOP FLOPS:

1. FIND the Verb and its helpers. Mark it in green or underline it twice.
2. LOCATE the Subject. Underline it.
3. FINISH the thought – Bracket the Complement.
4. LOSE the Prepositional Phrases. Parenthesize them. FIND, LOCATE, FINISH, AND LOSE.

How to Diagram

"Let's Eat Out Tonight" by Larry Kitchen

WHY USE COLOR?

When I was a child of four or five, my mother and I would often leave our home on Elm Street and walk to Main Street on a sunny afternoon. Sometimes our errands took us to Wilken's Dry Goods Store. Once inside, I would rush past the many bolts of fabrics in order to find and gaze at the display of colored threads.

This was a large, square exhibit of spools of thread, laid sideways, and displayed according to the color wheel. I still remember the joy I felt as I studied those shades and hues of the basic color wheel – red moved from pink to violet, yellow became orange, and blue slid from aquamarine to emerald green. All those shades of color in between – there were hundreds – way too many to count! How fortunate I felt to be able to see all those colors in one place! Seeing them made my day.

In fact, I can still visualize the many colors on that amazing thread display, and I still find joy in that memory.

In the same way, learning something as technical and abstract as parts of speech and sentence structure can be aided a great deal by adding something concrete – something like color.

You can visualize *blue*, but can you visualize a *preposition*?

For this reason I instituted the color system of diagramming.

> I hear, and I forget
>
> I see, and I remember
>
> I do, and I understand

THE SECRETS OF COLOR CODING:

1. ONLY FOUR COLORS EVER APPEAR ON THE BASELINE:

⭐	⭐	⭐	⭐
NOUN	PRONOUN	VERB	ADJECTIVE

(The NOUN and the PRONOUN are always interchangeable.)

2. ADJECTIVAL AND ADVERBIAL PHRASES ALWAYS APPEAR BELOW THE BASELINE:

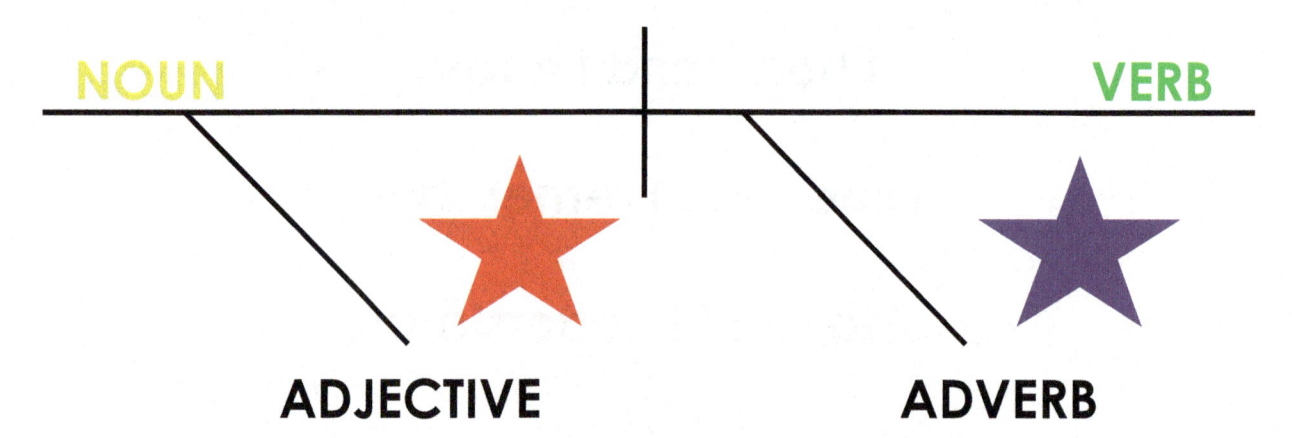

NOUN | VERB

ADJECTIVE ADVERB

3. PREPOSITIONAL PHRASES APPEAR BELOW THE BASELINE WHERE THEY ARE NEEDED. THOSE THAT MODIFY NOUNS (ADJECTIVAL) APPEAR UNDER THE NOUN; THOSE THAT MODIFY VERBS (ADVERBIAL) APPEAR UNDER THE VERB.

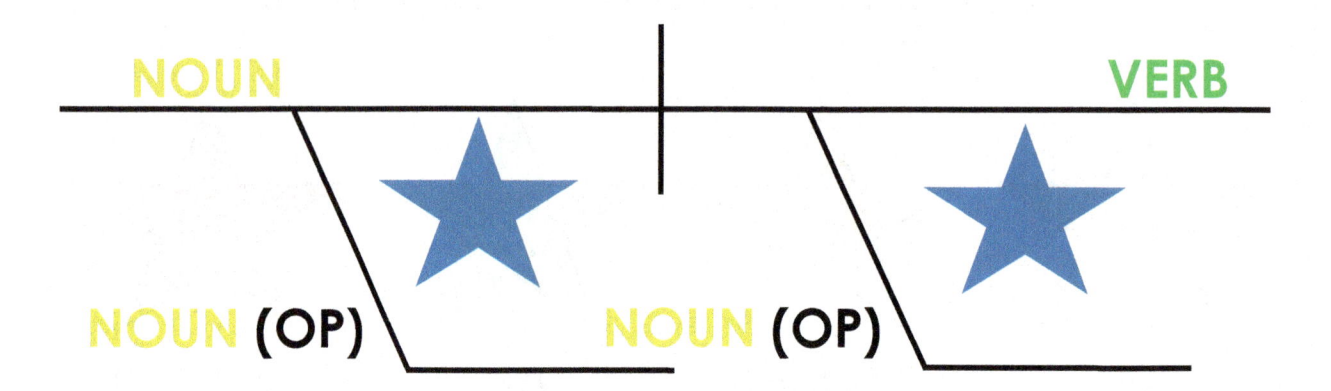

NOUN | VERB

NOUN (OP) | NOUN (OP)

ADJECTIVE PHRASE | **ADVERB PHRASE**

DIAGRAMMING INTRANSITIVE VERBS:

     S   **VI**   **PP**

Good <u>actions</u> **speak** (for themselves).

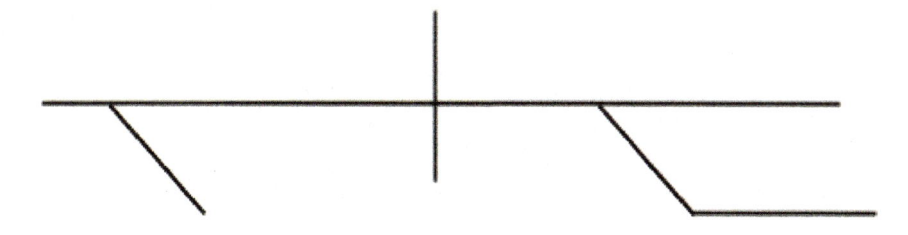

         S   **VI**

Pleasant <u>hours</u> **fly** fast.

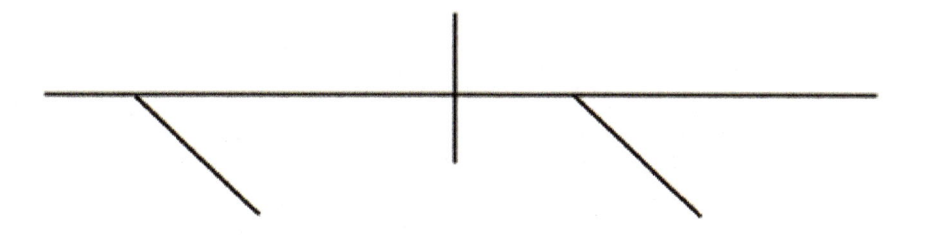

     S   **VI**   **PP**

<u>Spring</u> **is** (in my heart).

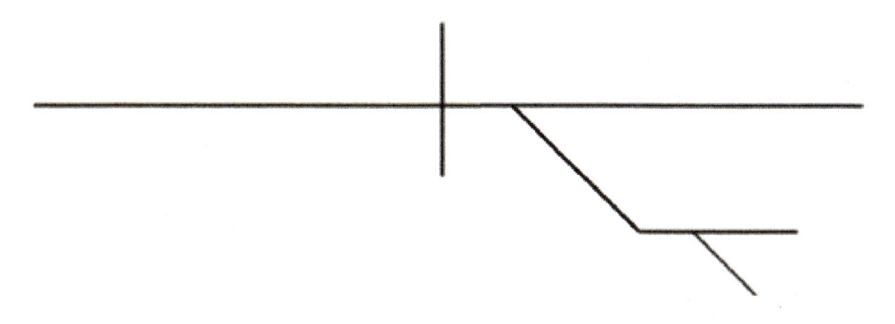

ANSWER KEY:

      S   VI   PP

Good <u>actions</u> **speak** (for themselves).

      S   VI

Pleasant <u>hours</u> **fly** fast.

      S   VI   PP

<u>Spring</u> **is** (in my heart).

DIAGRAMMING INTRANSITIVE VERBS:

     S   **VI**

A new <u>broom</u> **sweeps** clean.

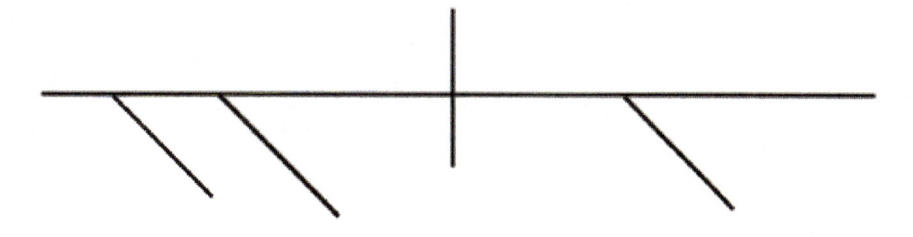

     S   **VI**

<u>Wisdom</u> **begins** (in wonder).

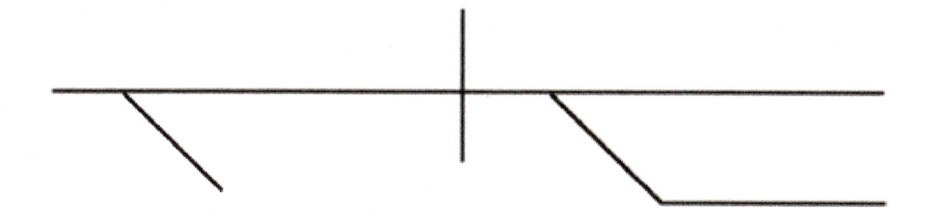

    PP   **VI**   **S**

(Out of difficulties) **grow** <u>miracles</u>.

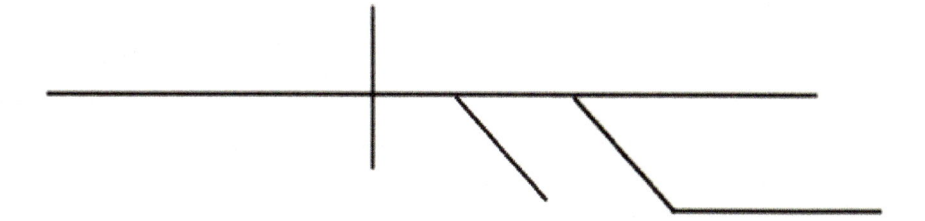

ANSWER KEY:

S   VI

A new <u>broom</u> **sweeps** clean.

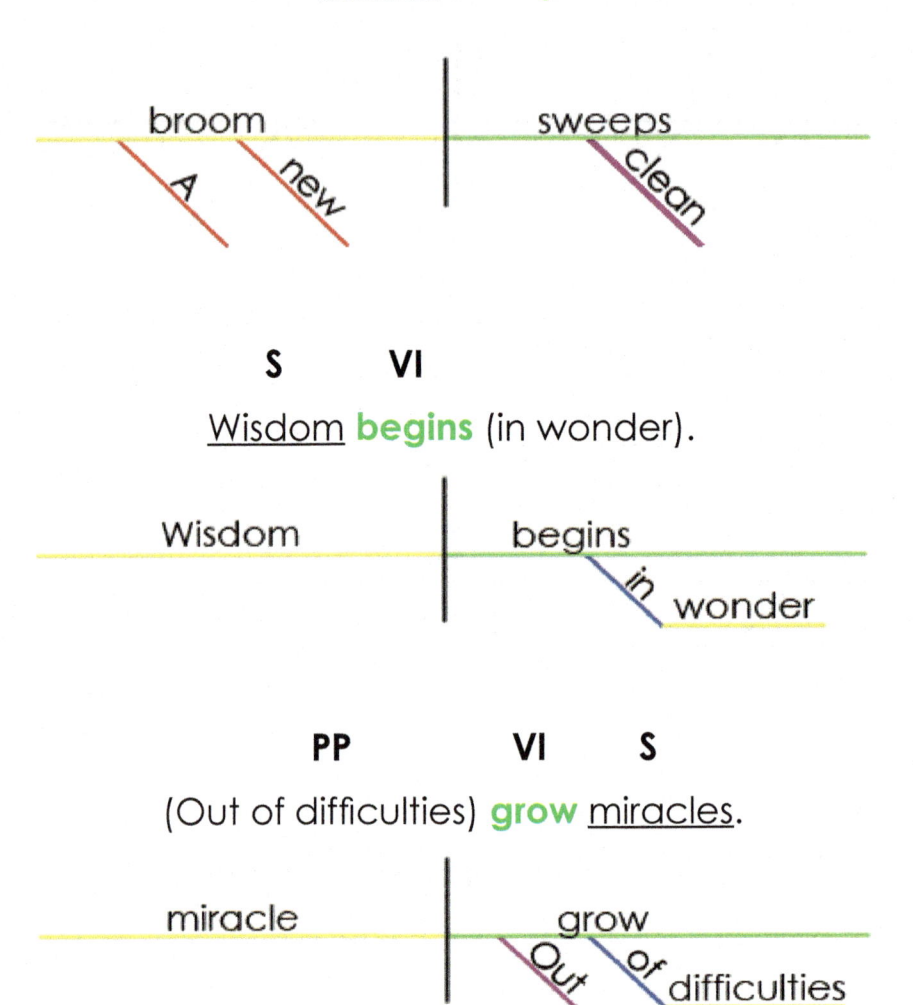

```
        broom  |  sweeps
       /   \   |      \
      A   new  |      clean
```

S   VI

<u>Wisdom</u> **begins** (in wonder).

```
   Wisdom     |   begins
              |      \in
              |         wonder
```

PP   VI   S

(Out of difficulties) **grow** <u>miracles</u>.

```
    miracle   |   grow
              |   /Out  \of
              |          difficulties
```

128

DIAGRAMMING LINKING VERBS:

S LV   PA
A good <u>deed</u> **is** never [lost].

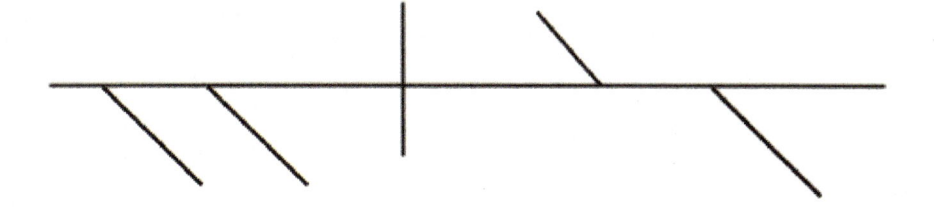

S LV   PN
A good <u>name</u> **is** a second [inheritance].

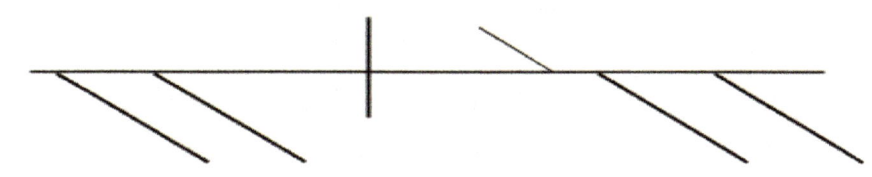

S   LV   PN
Great <u>possessions</u> **are** great [cares].

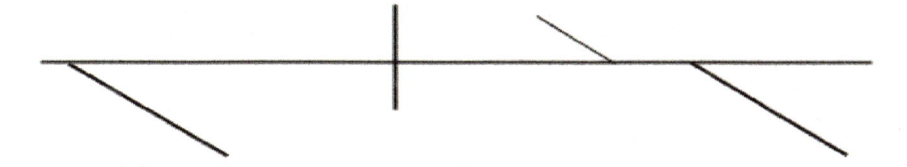

ANSWER KEY:

S LV   PA

A good <u>deed</u> **is** never [lost].

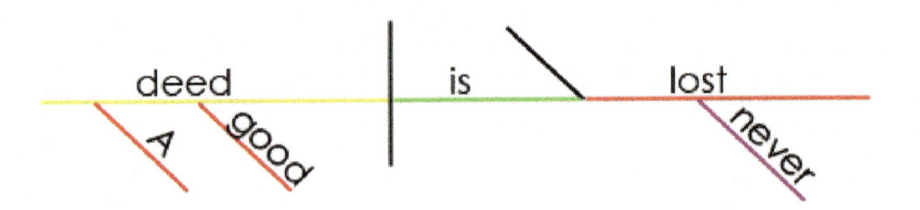

S LV   PN

A good <u>name</u> **is** a second [inheritance].

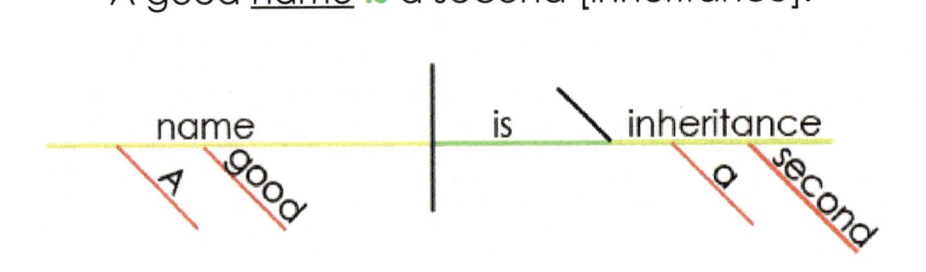

S LV   PN

Great <u>possessions</u> **are** great [cares].

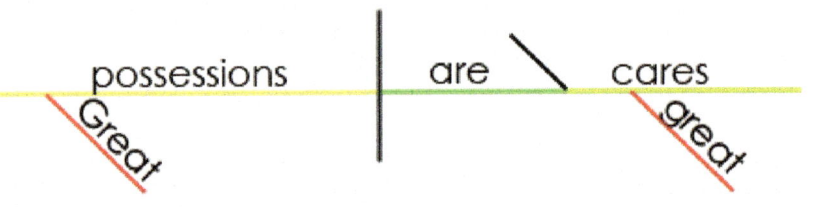

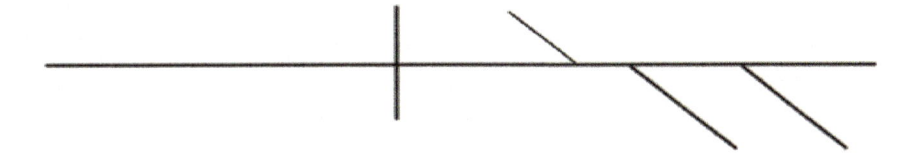

DIAGRAMMING LINKING VERBS:

S   S   LV   PN

<u>Liars</u> and <u>gossips</u> **are** Siamese [twins].

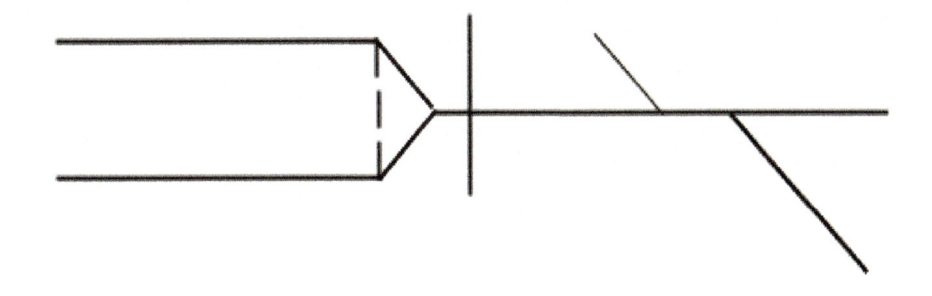

S   LV   PN   PP

<u>Obstinacy</u> **is** the [strength] (of the weak).

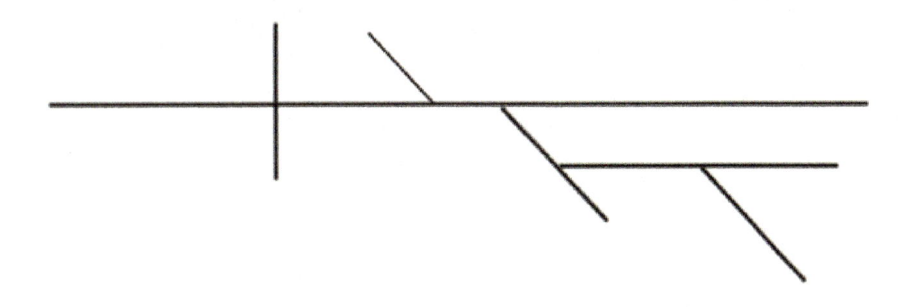

S   V   PN

<u>Self-defense</u> **is** nature's oldest [law].

ANSWER KEY:

S   S   LV   PN
Liars and gossips **are** Siamese [twins].

S   LV   PN   PP
Obstinacy **is** the [strength] (of the weak).

S   V   PN
Self-defense **is** nature's oldest [law].

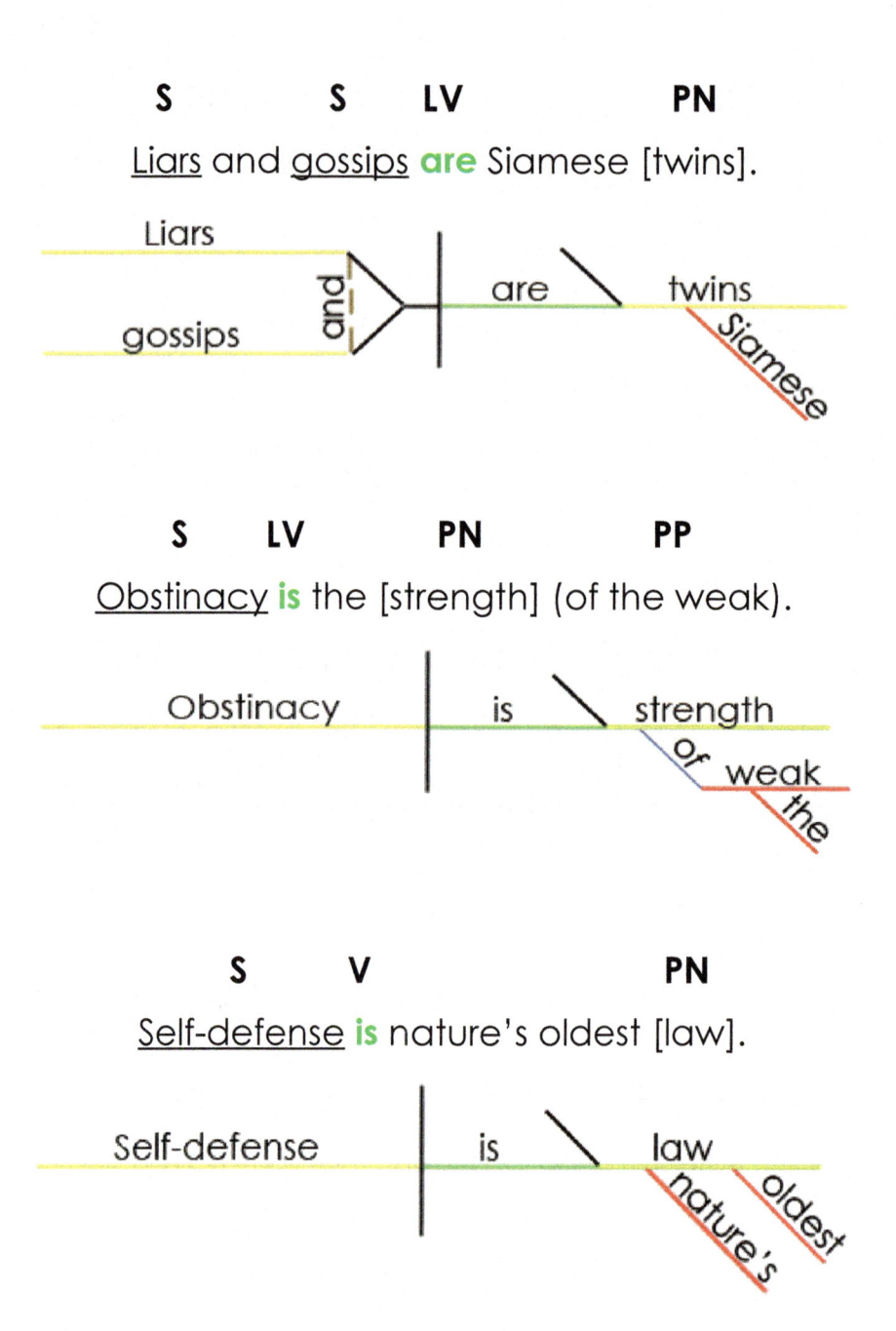

DIAGRAMMING ACTION VERBS:

S   AV   DO
A clean <u>conscience</u> **makes** a soft [pillow].

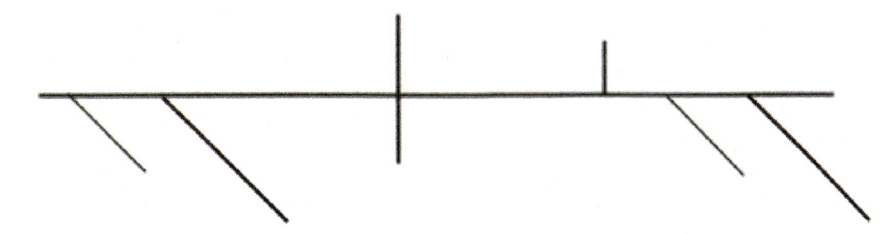

S   AV   DO
A small <u>leak</u> **will sink** a great [ship].

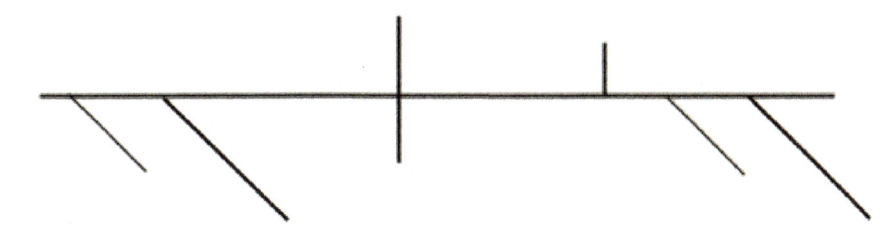

S   AV   DO
A small <u>body</u> **may harbor** a great [soul].

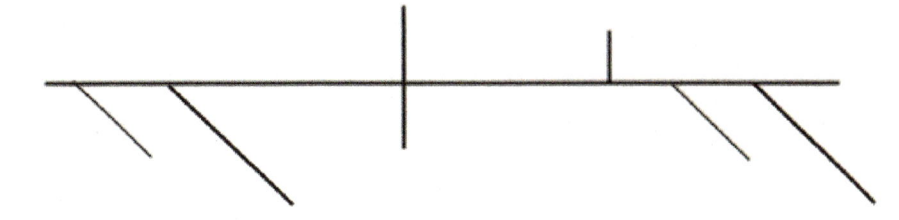

ANSWER KEY:

      S   **AV**   **DO**

A clean <u>conscience</u> **makes** a soft [pillow].

      S   **AV**   **DO**

A small <u>leak</u> **will sink** a great [ship].

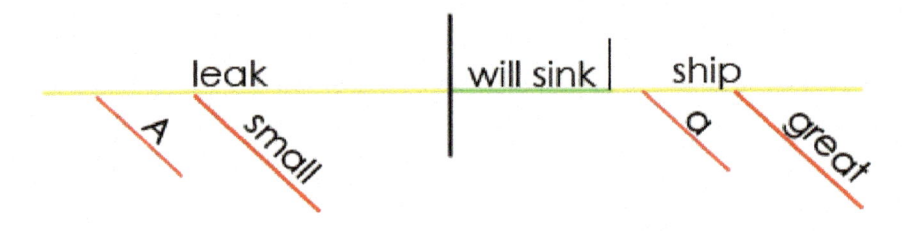

      S   **AV**   **DO**

A small <u>body</u> **may harbor** a great [soul].

DIAGRAMMING ACTION VERBS:

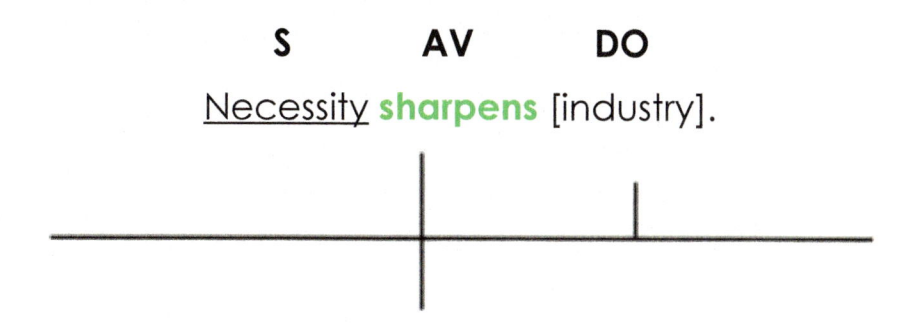

S   AV   DO
Necessity **sharpens** [industry].

S   AV   AV   DO
Promises **will** not **butter** any [bread].

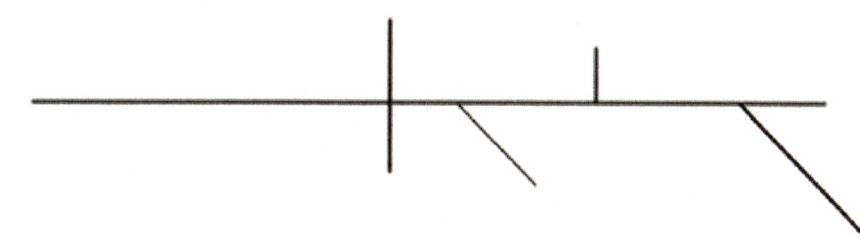

S   AV   AV   DO   PP
You **can** not **put** an old [head] (on young shoulders).

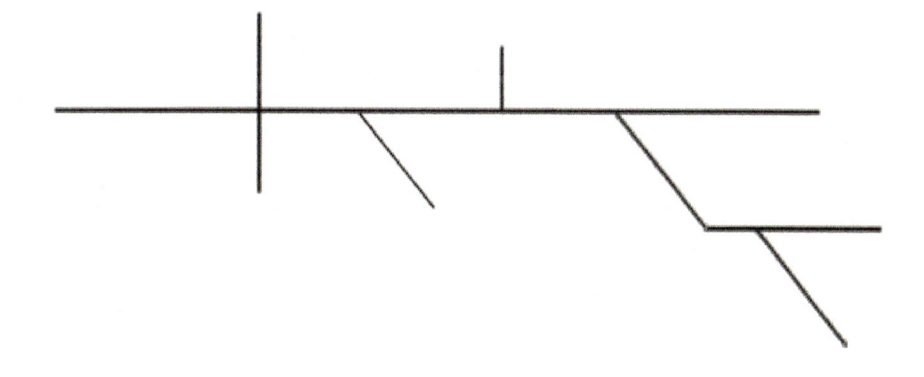

ANSWER KEY:

S   AV   DO

Necessity **sharpens** [industry].

| Necessity | sharpens | industry |

S   AV   AV   DO

Promises **will** not **butter** any [bread].

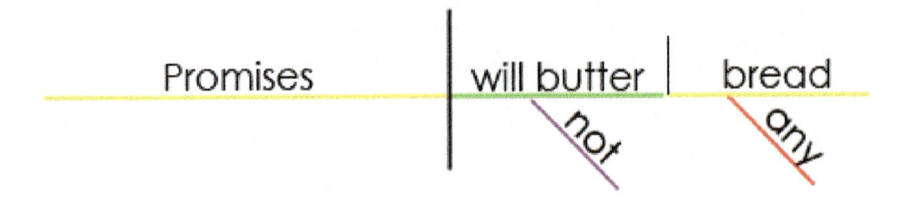

| Promises | will butter | bread |
                      not   *any*

S   AV   AV   DO   PP

You **can** not **put** an old [head] (on young shoulders).

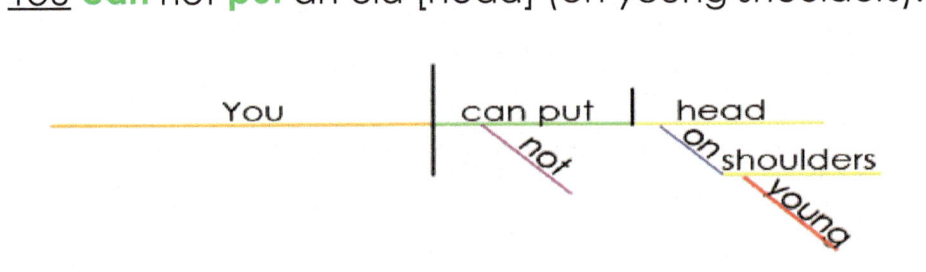

| You | can put | head |
             not   *on* shoulders
                          young

DIAGRAMMING LINKING, INTRANSITIVE, AND ACTION VERBS:

S LV   **PN**   **PP**

Envy **is** the sincerest [form] (of flattery).

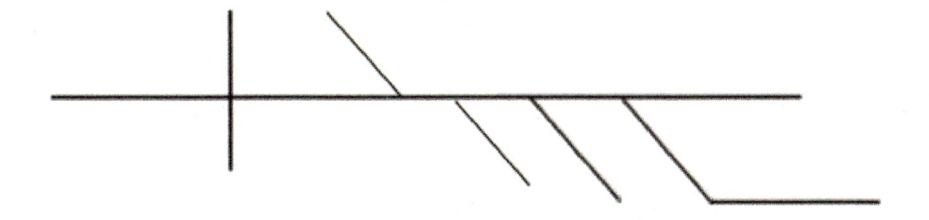

S VI   **PP**

Good health **is** (above wealth).

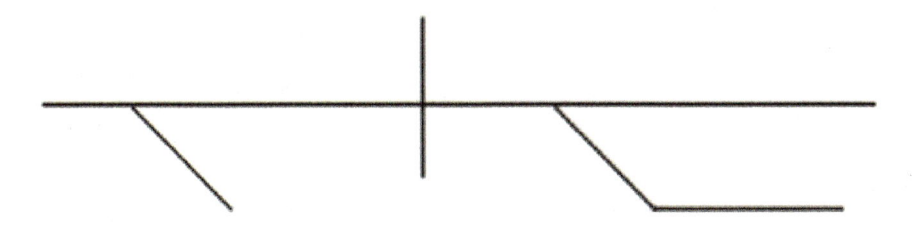

S AV   **DO**

Each day **provides** its own [gifts].

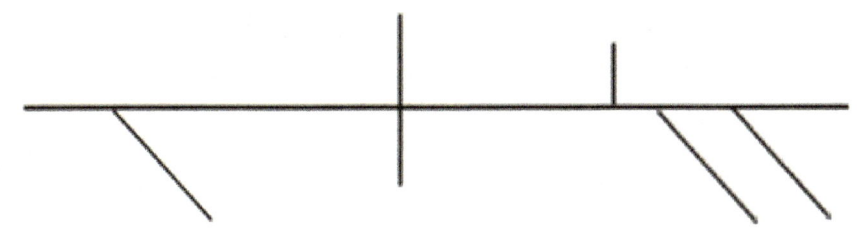

ANSWER KEY:

S LV   PN   PP
Envy **is** the sincerest [form] (of flattery).

S   VI   PP
Good health **is** (above wealth).

S   AV   DO
Each day **provides** its own [gifts].

DIAGRAMMING LINKING, INTRANSITIVE, AND ACTION VERBS:

S   AV   DO   PP
Ideas **shape** the [course] (of history).

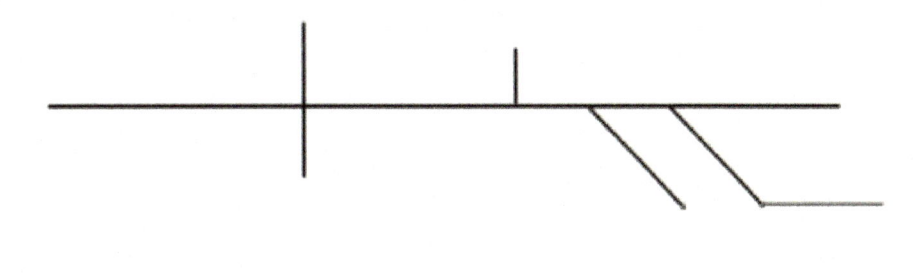

S   S   LV   PN
Fortune and misfortune **are** next-door [neighbors].

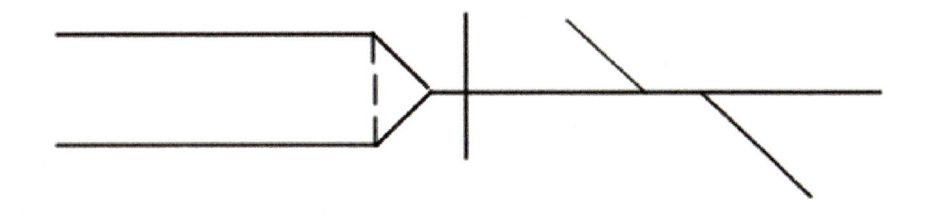

S   LV   PN
Every rule **has** an [exception].

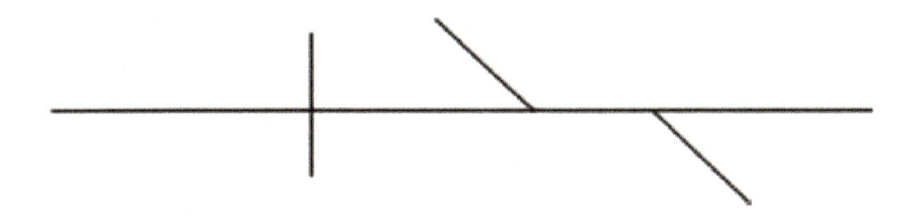

ANSWER KEY:

S   AV   DO   PP

<u>Ideas</u> **shape** the [course] (of history).

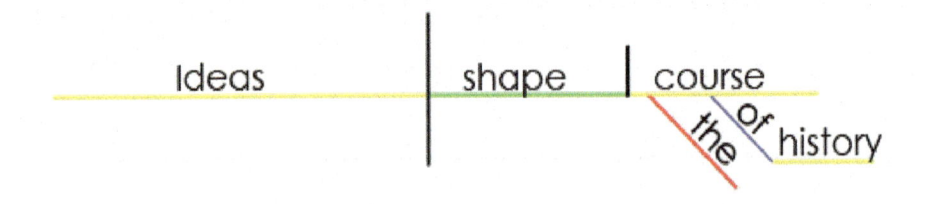

S   S   LV   PN

<u>Fortune</u> and <u>misfortune</u> **are** next-door [neighbors].

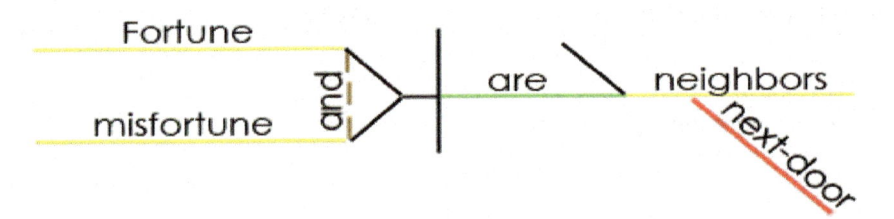

S   LV   PN

Every <u>rule</u> **has** an [exception].

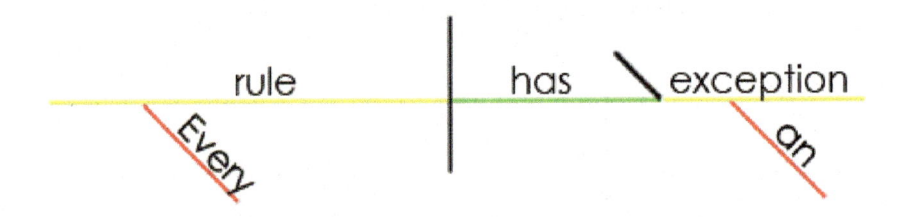

DIAGRAMMING LINKING, INTRANSITIVE, AND ACTION VERBS:

     S   **S**   **AV**   **DO**

A #2 <u>pencil</u> and a <u>dream</u> **can take** [you] anywhere.

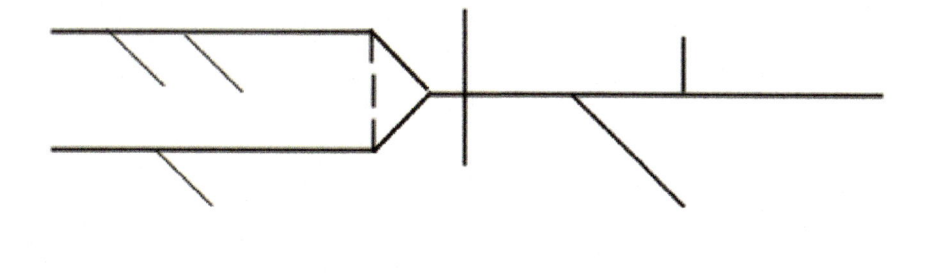

    S   **VI**   **S**   **VI**

<u>Nothing</u> **happens** until <u>something</u> **moves**.

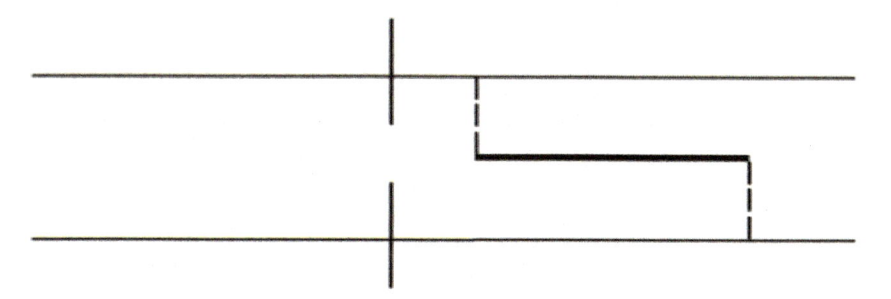

ANSWER KEY:

      S   **S**   **AV**   **DO**

A #2 <u>pencil</u> and a <u>dream</u> **can take** [you] anywhere.

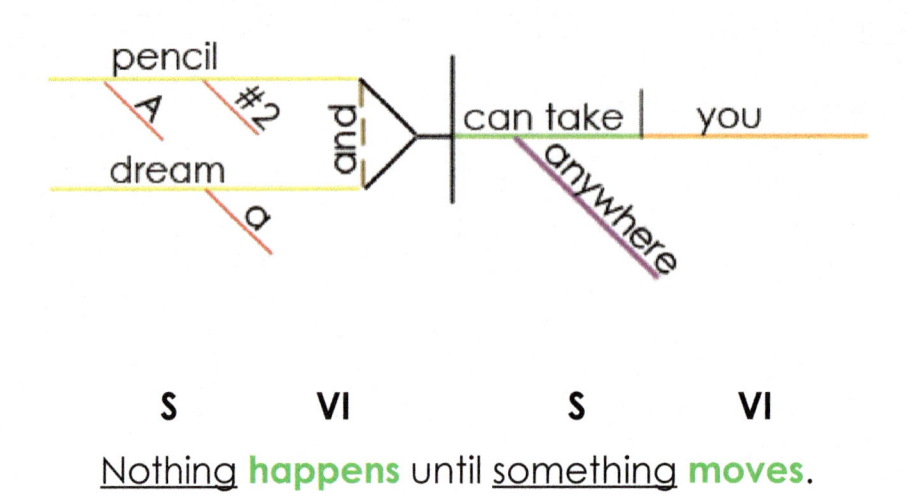

      S   **VI**   **S**   **VI**

<u>Nothing</u> **happens** until <u>something</u> **moves**.

(Notice: the words *something* and *nothing* are pronouns and should be marked in orange rather than yellow.)

DIAGRAMMING INDIRECT OBJECTS:

S   AV   IO   DO

King Constantine **bought** {Prince Sergio Paulo} a [pony].

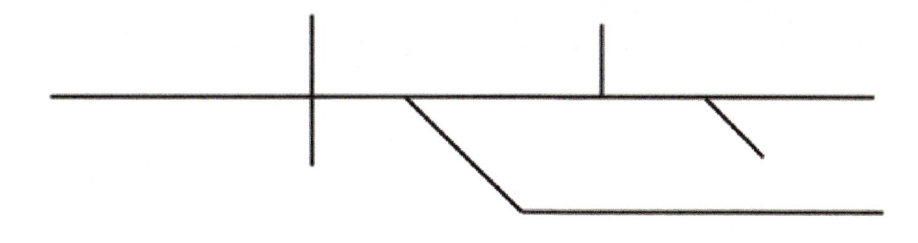

S   AV   IO   DO

King Constantine **paid** the {seller} [five-hundred dollars].

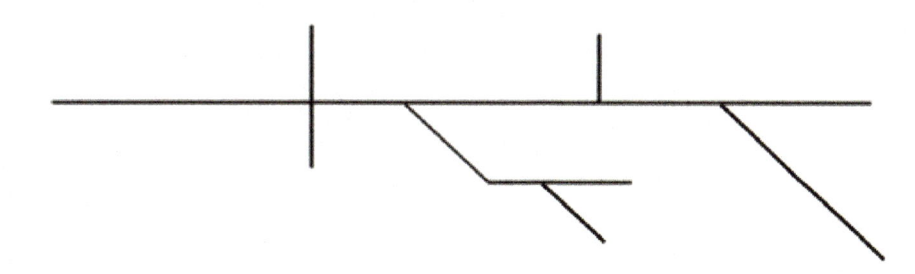

S   AV   IO   DO   PP

Prince Sergio Paulo **gave** his {pony} the [name] (of Jack).

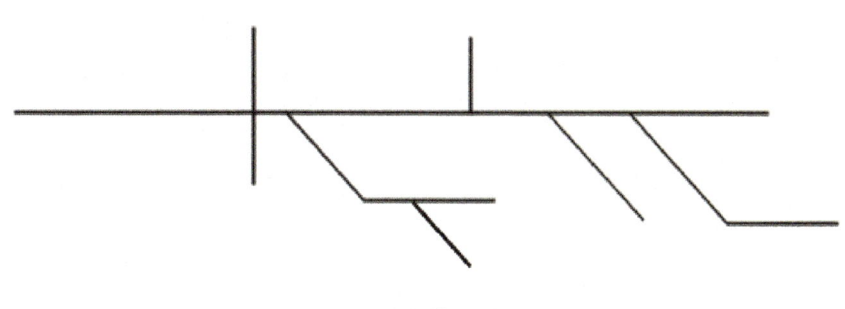

ANSWER KEY:

S **AV** **IO** **DO**

King Constantine **bought** {Prince Sergio Paulo} a [pony].

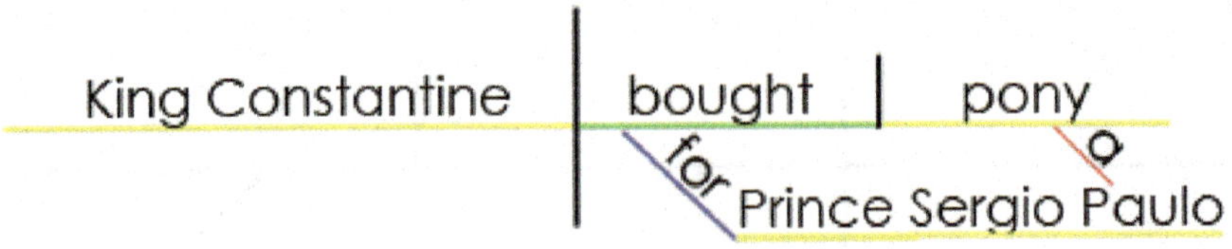

S **AV** **IO** **DO**

King Constantine **paid** the {seller} [five-hundred dollars].

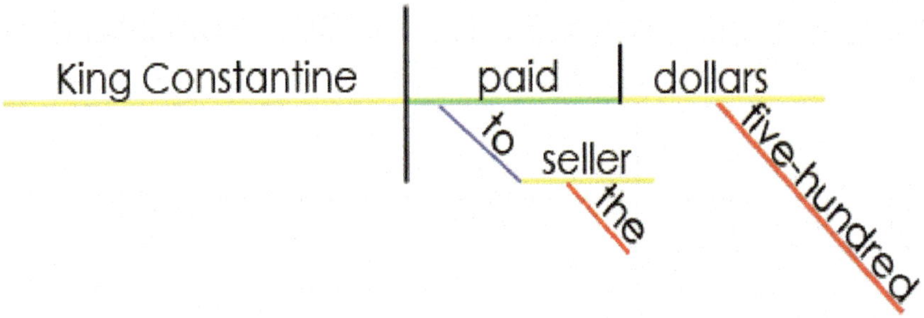

S **AV** **IO** **DO** **PP**

Prince Sergio Paulo **gave** his {pony} the [name] (of Jack).

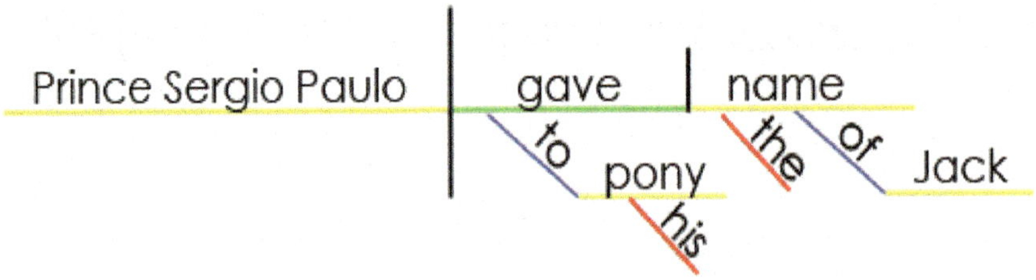

DIAGRAMMING MORE INDIRECT OBJECTS:

S   AV   IO   DO   PP

Sergio always **gave** {Jack} a [rubdown] (after exercise).

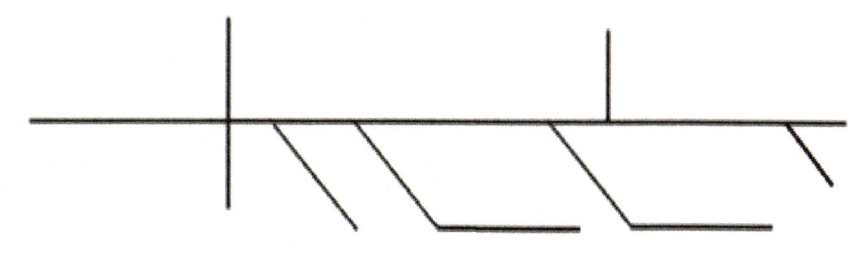

S   AV   IO   DO

Lady Cassandra **gave** {Nessa} the Latin [award].

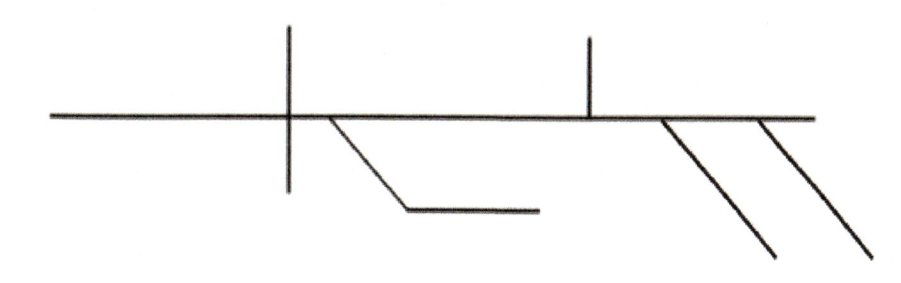

S   AV   IO   DO

The coachman **brought** the {King} [his new carriage.]

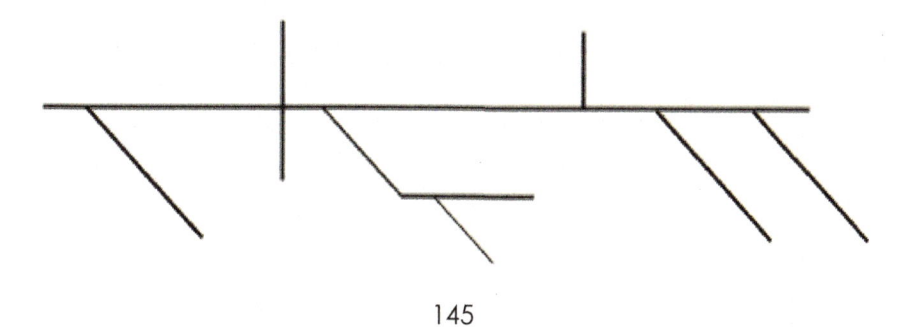

ANSWER KEY:

S AV IO DO PP
Sergio always **gave** {Jack} a [rubdown] (after exercise).

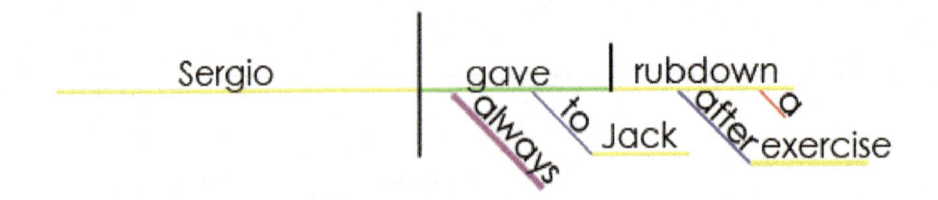

```
Sergio        | gave    | rubdown
         always   to Jack   a   after exercise
```

S AV IO DO
Lady Cassandra **gave** {Nessa} the Latin [award].

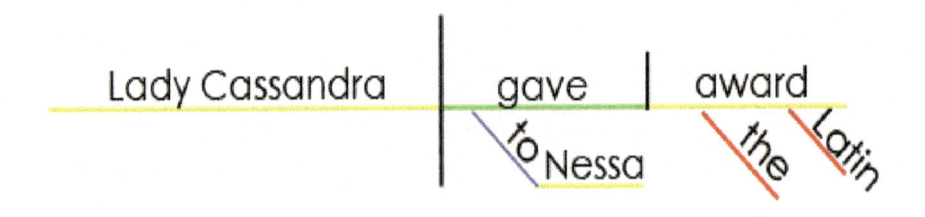

```
Lady Cassandra | gave  | award
                 to Nessa  the  Latin
```

S AV IO DO
The coachman **brought** the {King} [his new carriage.

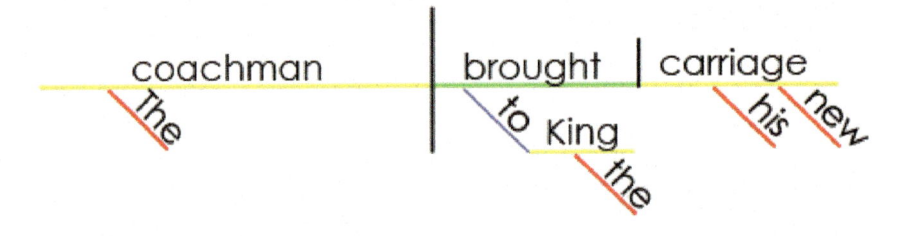

```
coachman      | brought | carriage
 The            to King    his  new
                the
```

DIAGRAMMING OBJECTIVE COMPLEMENTS

Here are three things to remember about the
Objective Complement (OC):

1. It **completes** the sentence, and it **appears after the Direct Object (DO)**.

2. It will be a **NOUN** or an **ADJECTIVE**.

3. If it is a **NOUN**, it **renames** the direct object **(DO)**. If it is an **ADJECTIVE**, it **describes** the direct object **(DO)**.

DIAGRAM THE FOLLOWING SENTENCE USING OBJECTIVE COMPLEMENTS:

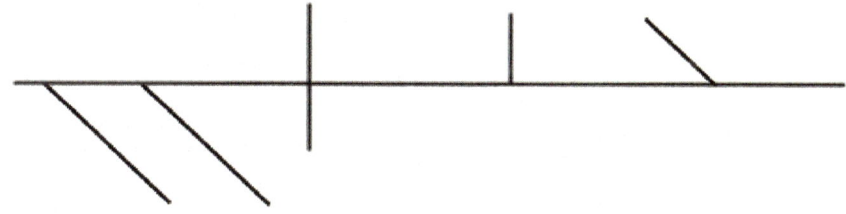

              S   AV   DO   OC [N]
The girls' brother **named** the [pony] {Jack}.

Find the Answer on Page 149

PLEASE NOTICE:

The last word on the **baseline** is the **Objective Complement (OC)**. This word is preceded by a **slanting line**. The **slanting line** points back to the **Direct Object(DO)**. In this way it shows us that the **Direct Object (DO)** is not complete without the **Objective Complement (OC)**. The **Objective Complement(OC) renames**(as a **NOUN**) or **explains**(as an **ADJECTIVE**) the **Direct Object (DO)**.

DIAGRAMMING OBJECTIVE COMPLEMENTS:

S   AV   DO   OC [N]
Gussie **called** [him] {Lord Jack}.

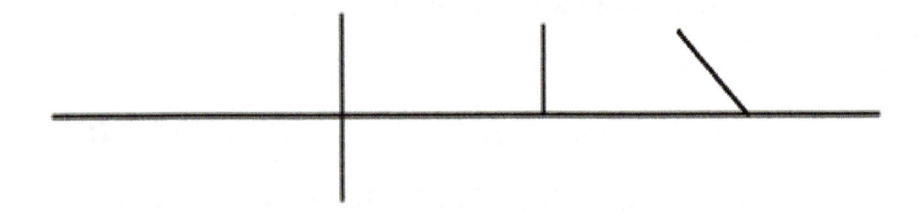

S   AV   DO   OC [A]
The saddle pad **kept** [Jack] {comfortable}.

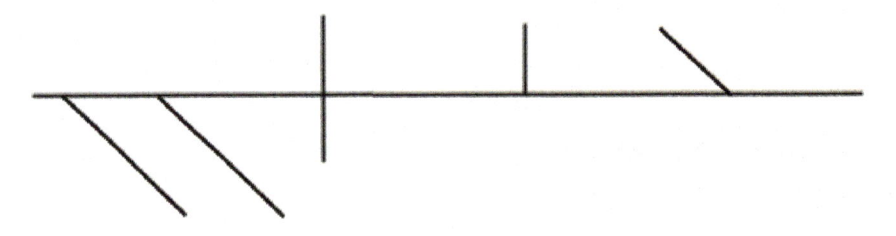

ANSWER KEY:

       S   **AV**   **DO** **OC [N]**

The girls' <u>brother</u> **named** the [pony] {Jack}.

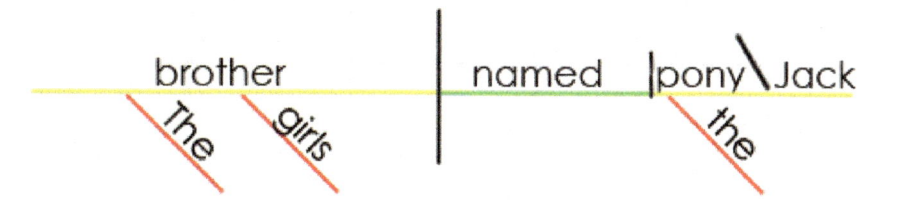

```
    brother   |  named  | pony \ Jack
   \The \girls             \the
```

    S   **AV**   **DO**   **OC [N]**

<u>Gussie</u> **called** [him] {Lord Jack}.

```
   Gussie | called | him  \ Lord Jack
```

    S   **AV**   **DO**   **OC [A]**

The saddle <u>pad</u> **kept** [Jack] {comfortable}.

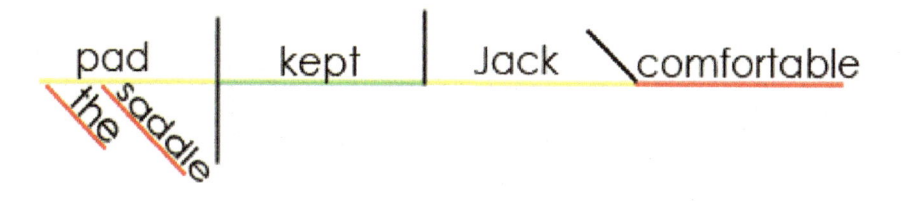

```
    pad    |  kept  |  Jack  \ comfortable
  \the \saddle
```

DIAGRAMMING OBJECTIVE COMPLEMENTS:

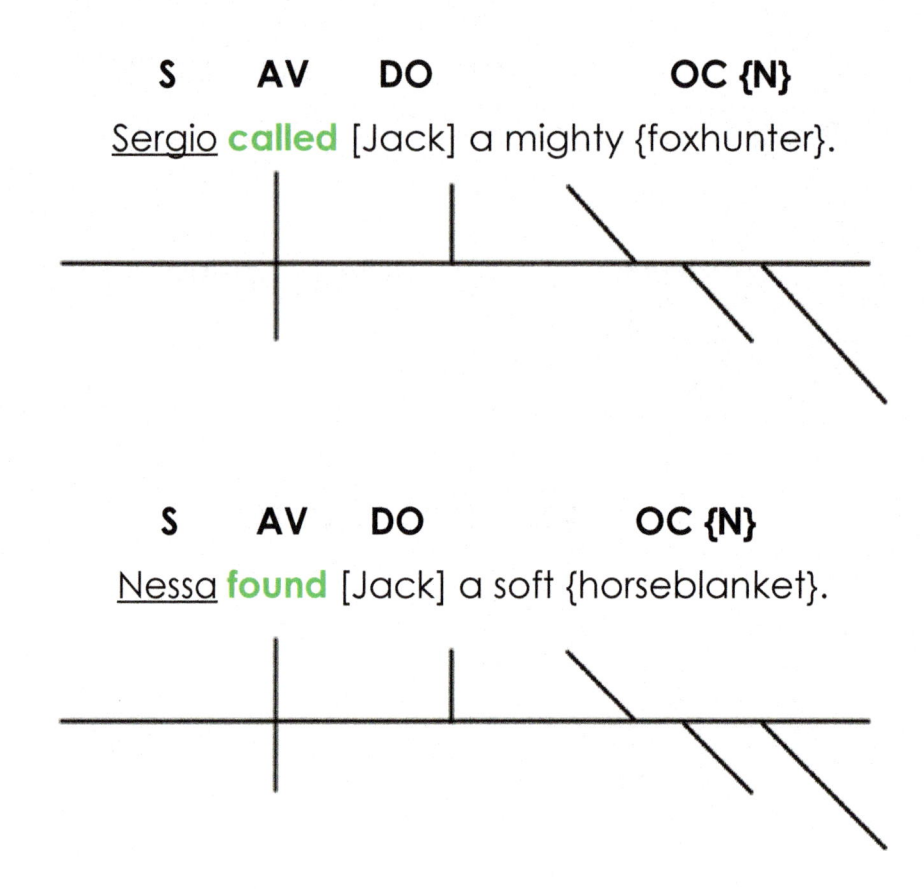

     S   **AV**   **DO**   **OC {N}**

Sergio **called** [Jack] a mighty {foxhunter}.

     S   **AV**   **DO**   **OC {N}**

Nessa **found** [Jack] a soft {horseblanket}.

ANSWER KEY:

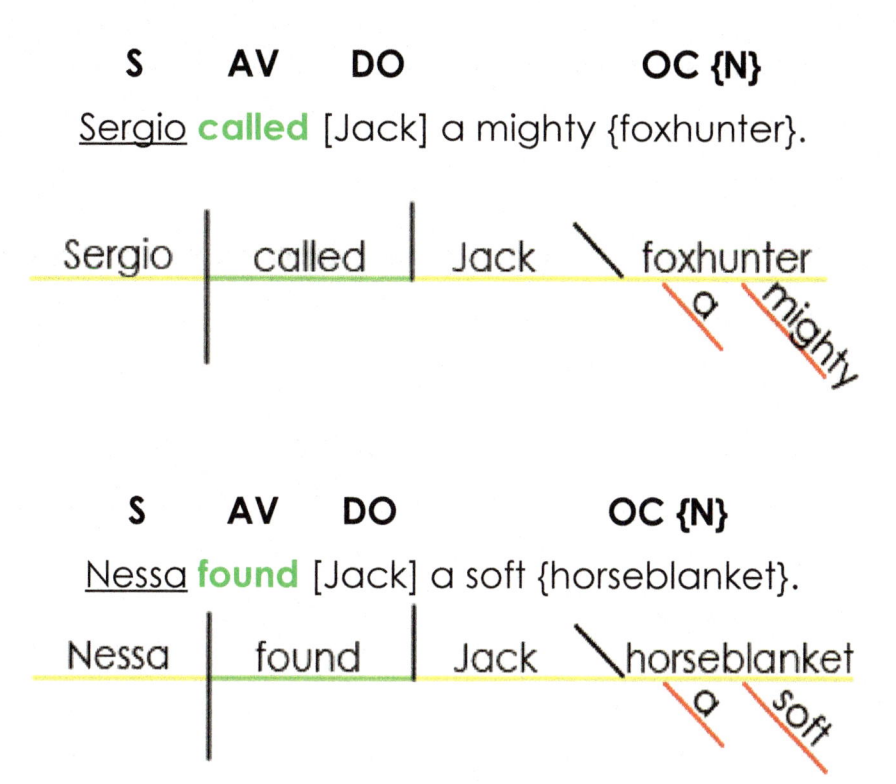

S   AV   DO   OC {N}

Sergio **called** [Jack] a mighty {foxhunter}.

Diagram: Sergio | called | Jack \ foxhunter (with "a" and "mighty" on slanted lines under foxhunter)

S   AV   DO   OC {N}

Nessa **found** [Jack] a soft {horseblanket}.

Diagram: Nessa | found | Jack \ horseblanket (with "a" and "soft" on slanted lines under horseblanket)

THE VERB PHRASE:

A phrase is **a group of related words**. In this book we introduce three types of phrases, the noun phrase, the verb phrase, and the prepositional phrase.

The verb phrase consists of **a main verb and all its helpers**. Here is an example: Marceline has been being teased lately by Smokey.

The words in green make up the **verb phrase**. Words that you have come to recognize as linking verbs are also used as helping verbs.

For Your Information, here is a list of the helping verbs: am, is, are, was, were, be, being, been, have, has, had, do does, did, shall, will, should, would, may, might, must, can, could.

MORE INFORMATION ON PHRASES:

1. Phrases do NOT have subjects and verbs – they are **a group of related words.**

2. A NOUN PHRASE is a noun and its helpers. (as in "a famous American artist".)

3. A VERB PHRASE is a verb and its helpers. (as in "should have been writing.")

4. A PREPOSITIONAL PHRASE is a preposition and its helpers. (as in over the rainbow, upon my shoulder, or under the bridge.)

DIAGRAMMING THE VERB PHRASE

      S   **VI**   **PP**

Lady Cassandra **will be listening** (for the gong).

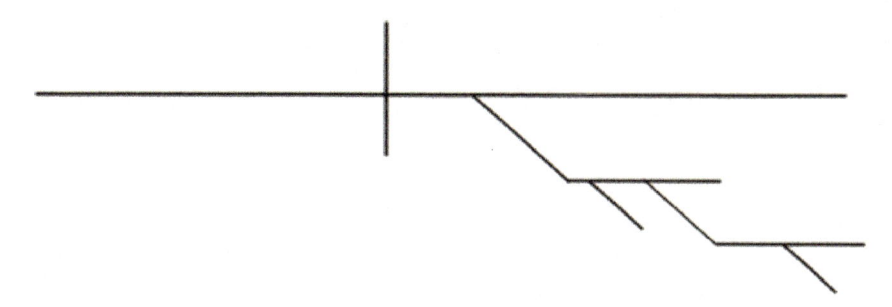

    S   **VI**   **PP**   **PP**

Mrs. Grimm **must be asked** (for the key) (to the closet).

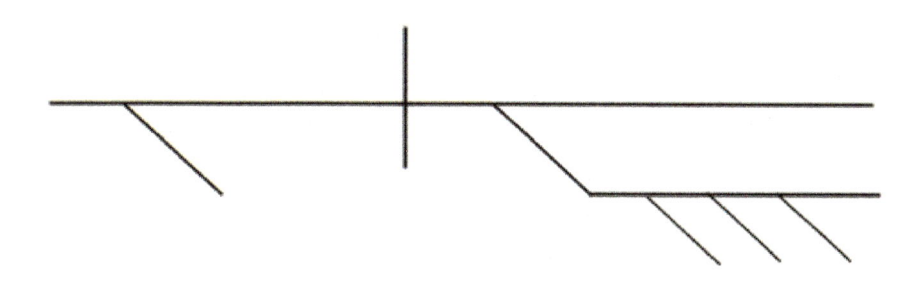

     S   **VI**   **PP**

The girls **have been playing** (with their new roller skates).

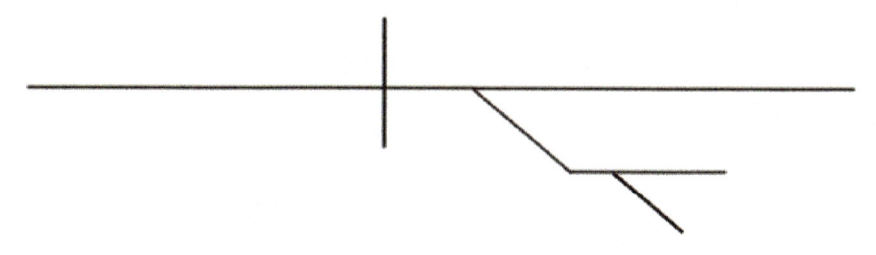

ANSWER KEY:

```
   S              VI               PP
Lady Cassandra will be listening (for the gong).
```

Lady Cassandra | will be listening
                                           for gong / the

```
   S           VI            PP          PP
Mrs. Grimm must be asked (for the key) (to the closet).
```

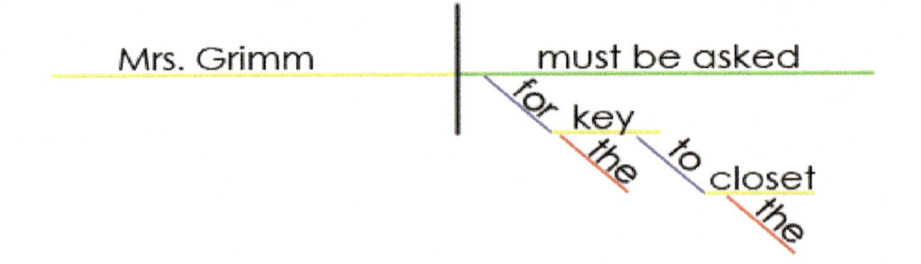

Mrs. Grimm | must be asked
                                     for key / the   to closet / the

```
   S          VI                          PP
The girls have been playing (with their new roller skates).
```

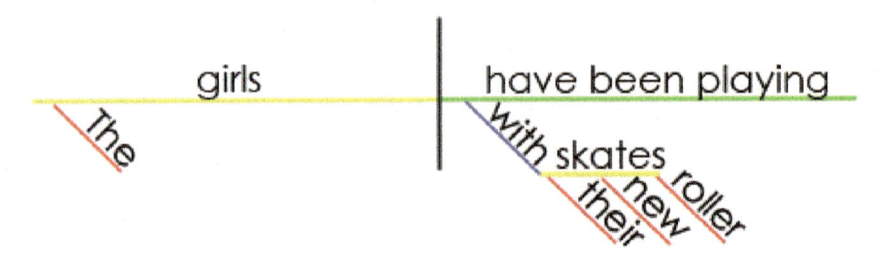

girls | have been playing
The   with skates / their / new / roller

THE PREPOSITIONAL PHRASE:

     S   **AV**   **DO**   **PP**

Only true <u>friends</u> **will leave** footprints (on your heart).

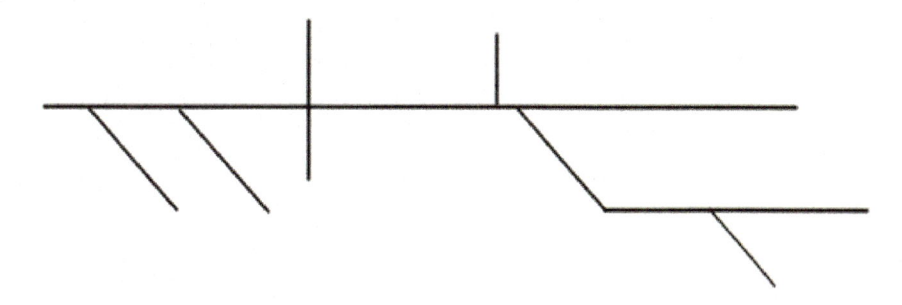

    S   **LV**   **PA**   **PP**

Every <u>field</u> **looks** [green] (from a distance).

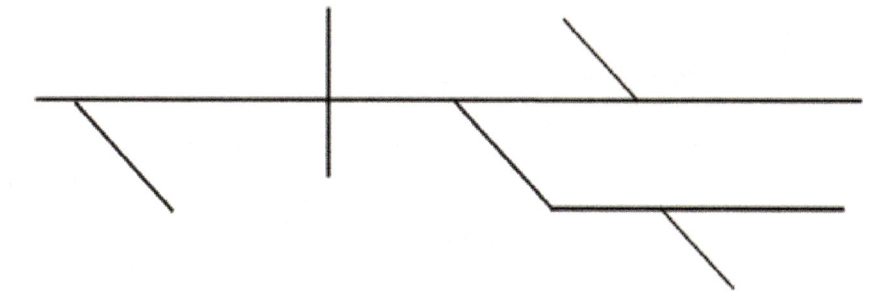

ANSWER KEY:

S   AV   DO   PP

Only true <u>friends</u> **will leave** footprints (on your heart).

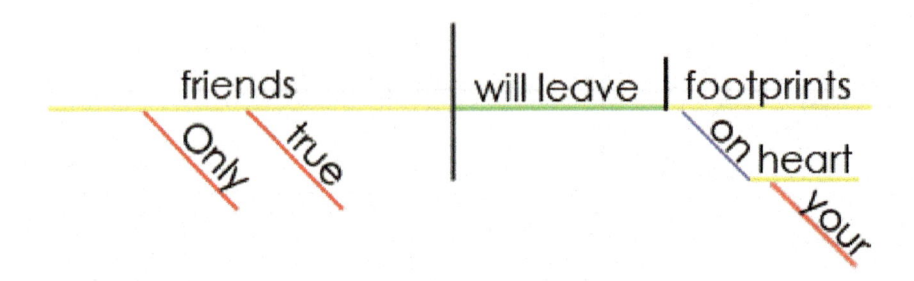

S   LV   PA   PP

Every <u>field</u> **looks** [green] (from a distance).

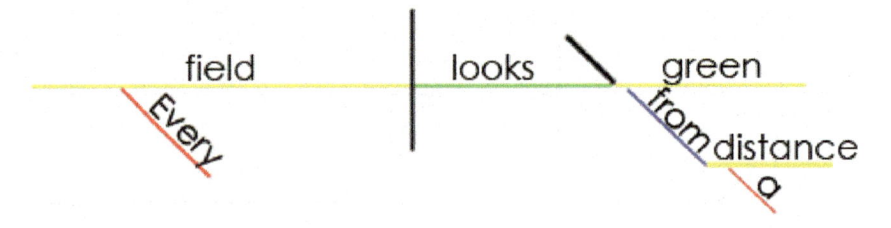

DIAGRAMMING PREPOSITIONAL PHRASES:

S AV DO   PP

<u>Fools</u> **use** [bets] (for arguments).

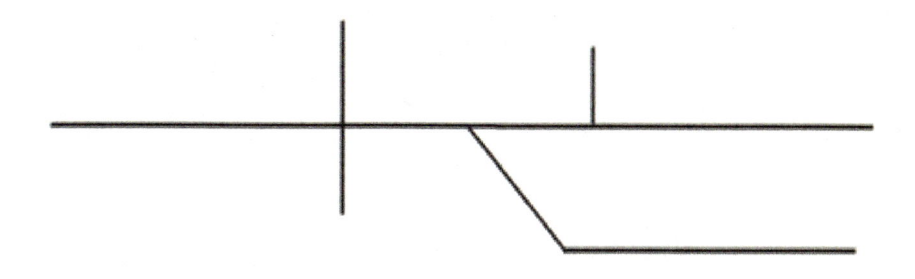

S   LV   PN   PP

<u>Punctuality</u> **is** the [key] (to success).

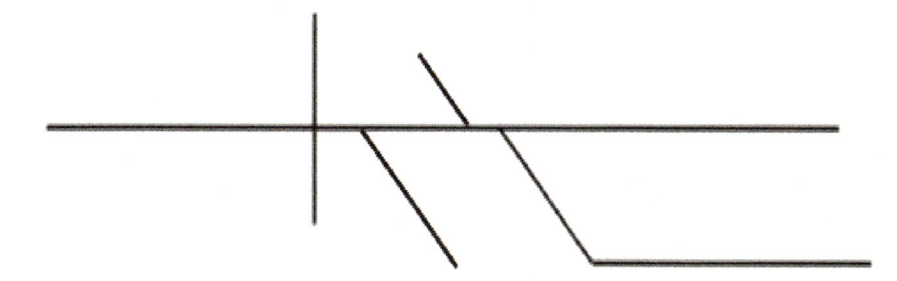

ANSWER KEY:

S   AV   DO   PP

Fools use [bets] (for arguments).

```
Fools  |  use  |  bets
                  \for
                    arguments
```

S   LV   PN   PP

Punctuality is the [key] (to success).

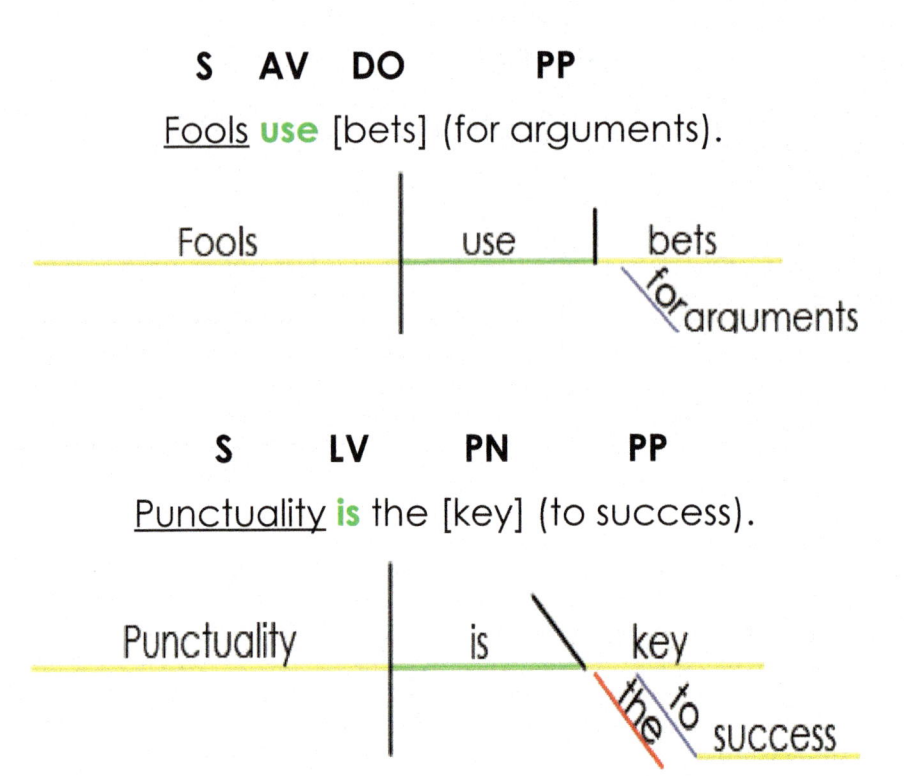

```
Punctuality  |  is  \  key
                    the \to
                          success
```

DIAGRAMMING ADJECTIVES AND ADVERBS:

ADJECTIVES usually cluster around the **NOUN**, while **ADVERBS** generally cluster around the **VERB**. **ADVERBS** often end in **-LY**.

Place all **ADJECTIVES** under the **NOUNS**, and place all **ADVERBS** under the **VERBS** on the baseline.

PREPOSITIONAL PHRASES ARE USED AS ADJECTIVES AND ADVERBS:

PREPOSITIONAL PHRASES will appear either under the **NOUN** or under the **VERB** on the baseline.

If the **PREPOSITIONAL PHRASE** answers one of these questions, it is an **ADJECTIVAL PHRASE**: **what kind? which one? what color? how many? whose?** Place this phrase **under** the **NOUN**.

If the **PREPOSITIONAL PHRASE** answers one of these questions, it is an **ADVERBIAL PHRASE**: **where? when? how? how often? to what extent?** Place this phrase **under** the **VERB**.

DIAGRAMMING ADJECTIVES AND ADVERBS:

ADJ ADJ   N   ADV   V   ADJ   N   PP
The brown cow proudly wore silver [bells] (around her neck).

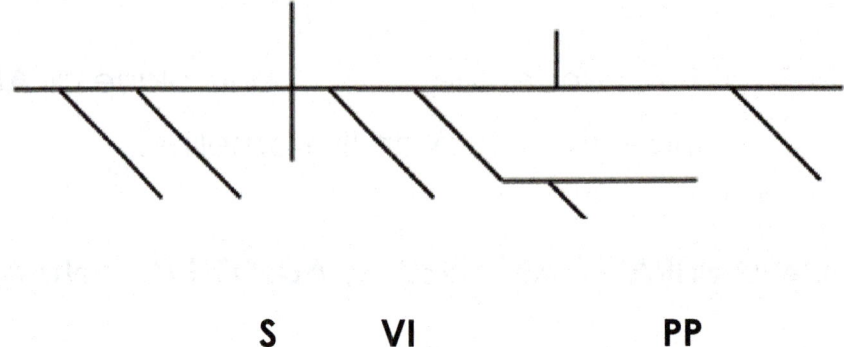

              S   VI   PP
The dark grey stone sparkled (in the bright sunshine).

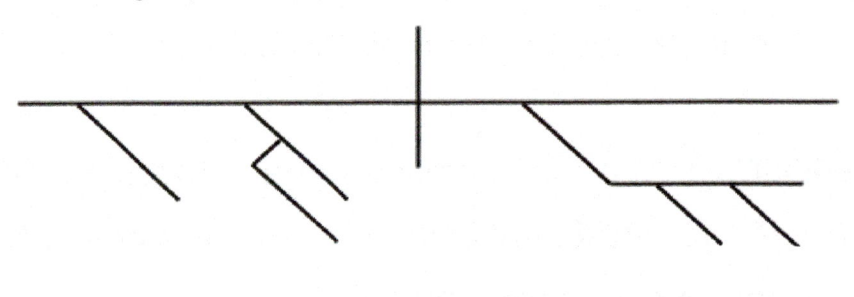

              S   PP   VI   PP
The shiny green leaves (of the pear tree) dropped (at our feet).

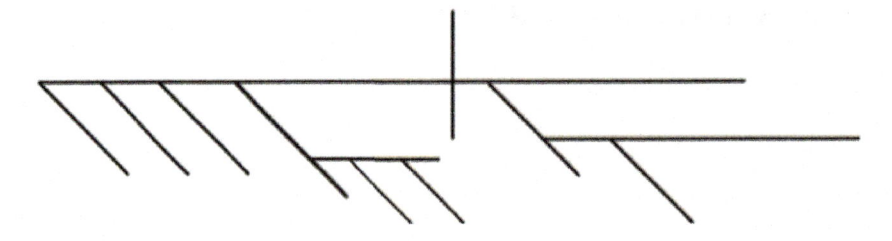

ANSWER KEY:

ADJ ADJ N   ADV V ADJ N   PP
The brown cow proudly **wore** silver [bells] (around her neck).

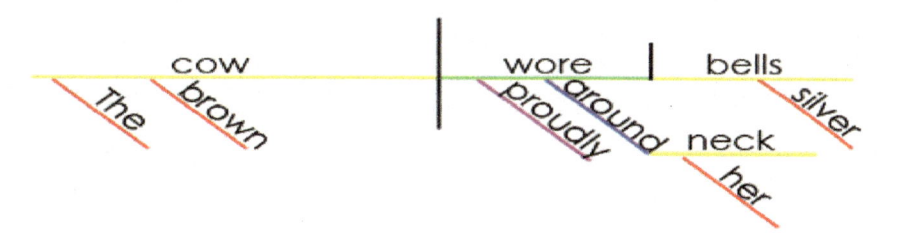

        S   VI   PP
The dark grey stone **sparkled** (in the bright sunshine).

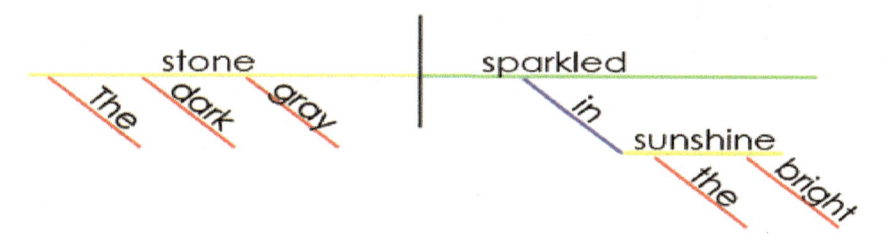

       S   PP   VI   PP
The shiny green leaves (of the pear tree) **dropped** (at our feet).

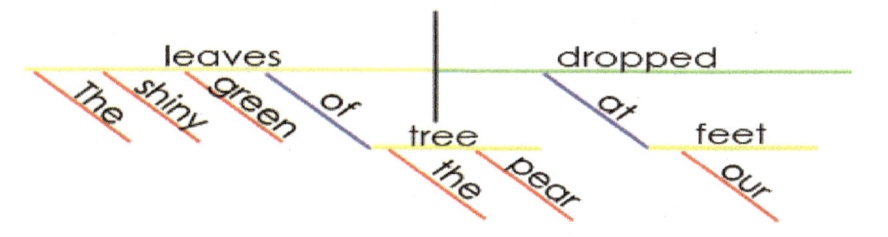

DIAGRAMMING ADJECTIVES AND ADVERBS:

S   AV   DO
Swirling white <u>snowflakes</u> **enveloped** the square [courtyard].

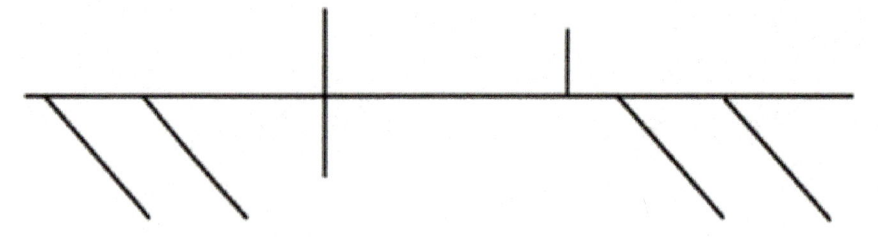

S   VI
Gussie's <u>pony</u> **jumped** quickly and easily.

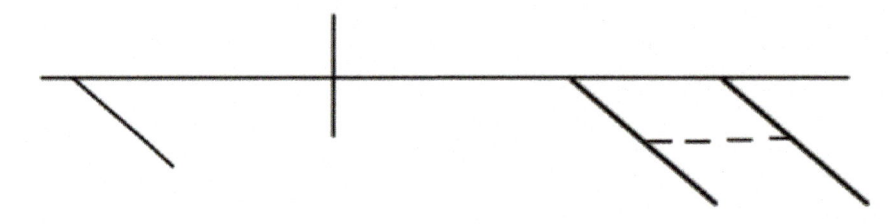

S   VI
Nessa's <u>pony</u> **stood** stubbornly and firmly.

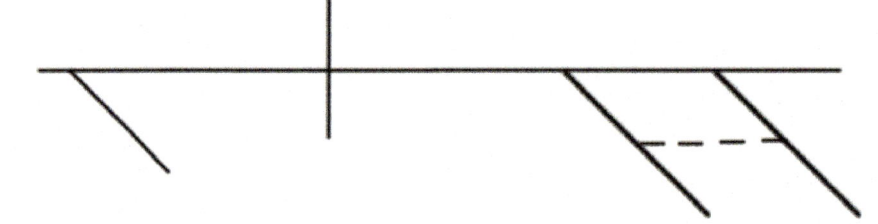

ANSWER KEY:

S   AV   DO

Swirling white <u>snowflakes</u> **enveloped** the square [courtyard].

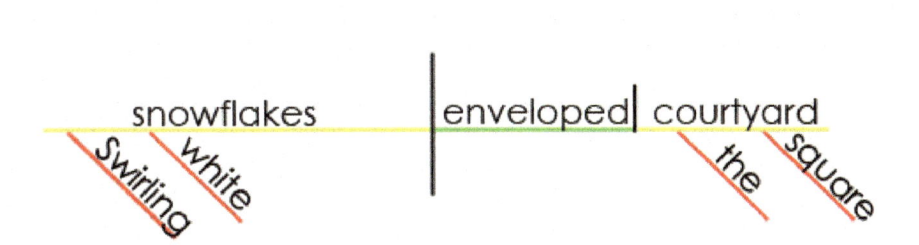

S   VI

Gussie's <u>pony</u> **jumped** quickly and easily.

S   VI

Nessa's <u>pony</u> **stood** stubbornly and firmly.

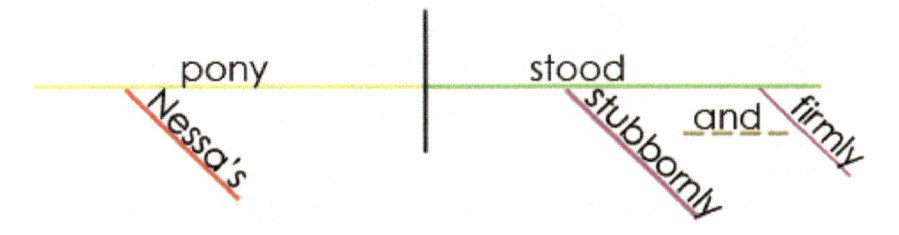

DIAGRAMMING ADJECTIVES AND ADVERBS:

    S   **VI**   **PP**

Smokey **crept** stealthily and softly [around the corner].

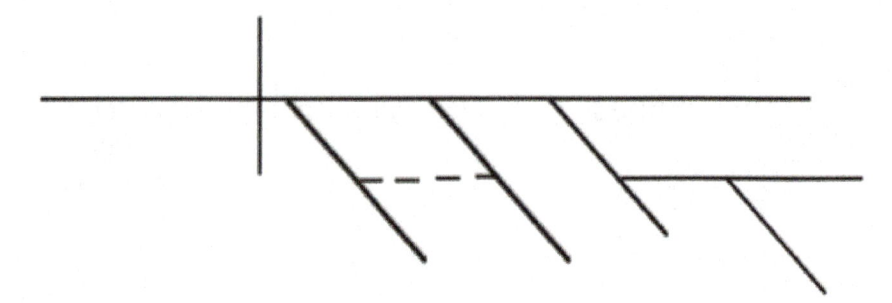

A PAGE FROM THE PALACE PICTURE ALBUM:

Jack at Play

ANSWER KEY:

```
  S      VI                                        PP
```
Smokey **crept** stealthily and softly [around the corner].

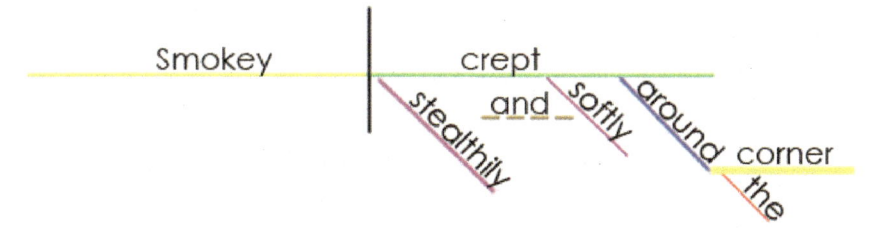

A PAGE FROM THE PALACE PICTURE ALBUM:

Emmeline   **Smokey**   **Marceline**

Glossary

"American Goldfinch in Winter" by Larry Kitchen

ADDITIONAL INFORMATION

THE SEVEN TYPES OF SENTENCES:

    S   VI

1. <u>Gussie</u> **searched**. (**VERB INTRANSITIVE**)

    S   AV   DO

2. <u>Gussie</u> **found** [Marceline]. (**ACTION VERB**)

    S   LV   PN

3. <u>Marceline</u> **is** Gussie's [cat] (**LINKING VERB**)

    S   LV   PA

4. <u>Gussie</u> **was** [clever]. (**LINKING VERB**)

    S   AV   IO   DO

5. <u>Gussie</u> **gave** {Marceline} a big [hug]. (**ACTION VERB**)

       S   AV   DO   OC (N)

6. <u>Queen Juliana</u> **named** [Gussie] {"The Feline Detective"}. (**ACTION VERB**)

    S   AV   DO OC (A)

7. <u>Gussie</u> **painted** **Marceline's** favorite [box] {blue}. (**ACTION VERB**)

HOW TO IDENTIFY A CLAUSE

What is the difference between a <u>phrase</u> and a <u>clause</u>?

A phrase – as you know – is simply **a group of related words.** The five most important phrases used in English are these: **verb** phrases, **prepositional** phrases, **participial** phrases, **infinitive** phrases, and **gerund** phrases. A clause, on the other hand, must have a **subject** and a **verb**. Actually, the word **'clause'** could be just another word for **'sentence'**. The difference is this: a **clause** may or may not stand alone, but a **sentence** must be able to stand alone; in other words, it must make perfect sense.

INDEPENDENT CLAUSES have a subject and a verb. They **can** stand alone.

DEPENDENT CLAUSES have a subject and a verb, but they **cannot** stand alone; they depend upon another clause in order to make sense.

HERE IS AN EXAMPLE OF AN INDEPENDENT CLAUSE:

I **walked** (to the store) (this morning).

HERE IS AN EXAMPLE OF A DEPENDENT CLAUSE:

After I **ate** my [breakfast].

Notice: Each clause has a subject and a verb, but **only one of them makes sense by itself.**

NOW LET'S COMBINE THE TWO:
After I ate my [breakfast], I walked (to the store) (this morning).

Voila! We have created a **COMPLEX SENTENCE.**

(A complex sentence is made up of one clause **that will stand alone** and one (or more) clauses **that will not stand alone.**)

THERE ARE FOUR TYPES OF SENTENCES:
1. SIMPLE
2. COMPOUND
3. COMPLEX
4. COMPOUND/COMPLEX

1. SIMPLE SENTENCES:

The <u>wind</u> **whispered** (through the pines).

The <u>moon</u> **shone** (over the lake).

The <u>air</u> **was** [heavy] (with the smell) (of honeysuckle).

(SIMPLE SENTENCES HAVE ONE COMPLETE THOUGHT.)

2. COMPOUND SENTENCES:

The <u>wind</u> **whispered** (through the pines), and <u>I</u> **played** my [guitar].

The <u>moon</u> **shone** (over the lake); <u>we</u> **walked** (to the beach), and <u>we</u> **followed** the [moonlight] (to our canoe).

The <u>air</u> **was** [heavy] (with the smell) (of honeysuckle), for <u>it</u> **was** the [month] (of June).

(COMPOUND SENTENCES HAVE TWO OR MORE COMPLETE THOUGHTS.)

3. COMPLEX SENTENCES:

After <u>I</u> **finished** my [homework], <u>I</u> **called** my friend [Erica].

Before <u>Erica</u> **answered** the [phone], <u>she</u> **turned** off her [computer].

Although <u>Erica</u> **was** [busy], <u>she</u> **closed** her [book] and **left** the [house] after <u>she</u> **brushed** her [hair].

(COMPLEX SENTENCES HAVE ONE COMPLETE THOUGHT AND TWO OR MORE INCOMPLETE THOUGHTS.)

4.COMPOUND/COMPLEX SENTENCES:

Jack **knows** that Erica **is going** (to the party); he **called** [us] yesterday before I **arrived** [home].

Erica **hopes** that Jack will **be** (at the party); he **had** not **told** his [brother] otherwise.

(COMPOUND SENTENCES HAVE TWO OR MORE COMPLETE THOUGHTS.)

THE GLOSSARY: A SHORT DICTIONARY OF GRAMMAR

ACTION VERB: (AV) An action verb expresses physical or mental action. Examples: walk, laugh, eat, jog (express physical action); trust, dream, imagine, appreciate (express mental action).

ADJECTIVE: An ADJECTIVE defines or changes (that is, modifies) the meaning of a NOUN or PRONOUN.

It answers the following questions: What kind? (brown eyes) Which one? (that girl) or how many? (a dozen doughnuts).

ADVERB: An ADVERB describes or modifies a VERB, an ADJECTIVE, AND an ADVERB.

It answers the following questions: How? (walked slowly) Where? (walked there) When? (walked then) Why? (walked for his health) and To What Extent? (walked far). An adverb often ends in *ly*.

APPOSITIVE: One or more words that rename or identify a NOUN or PRONOUN and appear next to it. Example: *Bill Nye the Science Guy stars on TV.* ("*the Science Guy*" is the appositive, renaming Bill Nye.)

CLAUSE: A group of words that form a complete thought (such as a simple sentence). A CLAUSE must have a SUBJECT and a VERB; a PHRASE does not have a SUBJECT and a VERB.

COMPLEMENT: From the Latin <u>complere</u>, meaning "to complete". The COMPLEMENT follows the MAIN VERB in the sentence and completes the basic thought.

COMPLEX SENTENCE: This type of sentence has one INDEPENDENT CLAUSE (a thought that WILL stand alone) and at least one DEPENDENT CLAUSE (a thought that WILL NOT stand alone.)

EXAMPLE: The boy became angry when his classmate hit him. (The conjunction when joins the two clauses. "The boy became angry" will stand alone. "when his classmate hit him" will not stand alone.)

COMPOUND SENTENCE: This sentence has two or more INDEPENDENT CLAUSES (both thoughts will stand alone).

EXAMPLE: I went clothes shopping; I didn't buy anything.

COMPOUND-COMPLEX SENTENCE: This sentence has at least TWO INDEPENDENT CLAUSES (complete statements that will stand alone) and at least ONE DEPENDENT CLAUSE (a statement that will not stand alone).

EXAMPLE: *The garage that Josh had built had only one bay, so he added a second one.* **"The garage had only one bay" stands alone. "He**

added a second one" stands alone. Both are INDEPENDENT CLAUSES. "that Josh had built" will not stand alone, so it is a DEPENDENT CLAUSE.

CONJUNCTIONS: These words join or link one part of a sentence to another. EXAMPLES: and, but, or, nor, for, yet.

EXAMPLES OF CONJUNCTIONS IN PAIRS: either. . .or, neither. . .nor, both. . .and, not only. . .but also.

EXAMPLES OF CONJUNCTIONS THAT INTRODUCE AN ADVERB CLAUSE: after, as, as if, in order that, since, although, unless, until, whenever, wherever, while.

DIAGRAMMING: A visual representation of how one part of a sentence relates to another.

DIRECT OBJECT: (DO) Any word acting as a NOUN or PRONOUN that receives the action of the VERB and completes the meaning of the sentence.

FRAGMENT: Part of the sentence; either the SUBJECT or some or all of the PREDICATE is missing.

GERUNDS: VERBS that end in *ing* and function as NOUNS.

HELPING VERBS: Verbs that help the MAIN VERB in a sentence to make a clear statement.

EXAMPLES: am, is, are, was, were, be, being, been; have, has, had; do, does, did; shall, will, should, would; may, might, must, can, could.

                           S   VI   PP

SENTENCE EXAMPLE: <u>Jennie</u> should be arriving (by Tuesday).

IDIOMS: Common, vigorous expressions that grew up with a language and are peculiar to it.

EXAMPLE IN ENGLISH: That skunk is *a stone's throw* away.

EXAMPLE IN GERMAN: That skunk is *a cat's jump* away.

(Another well-known English idiom is this one: Bring your umbrella; *it's raining cats and dogs!*)

INDIRECT OBJECTS (IO): NOUNS or PRONOUNS that complete the thought introduced by the VERB. They answer one of these questions: *for whom? to whom? for what? to what?*

              S   AV   IO   DO

EXAMPLE: Alfred gave his {teacher} an [apple]. (To whom did he give the apple? *He gave it to his teacher.*)

INFINITIVES: These are VERBALS that always appear preceded by the word *to*. They serve as NOUNS, ADJECTIVES, or ADVERBS in a sentence.

EXAMPLE: To err is human. *To err* is a VERBAL NOUN. It is still an ACTION VERB but it now acts as a NOUN, for it is the subject in this sentence.

INTERJECTIONS: Words that express powerful emotions such as happiness, grief, hate, or surprise. They stand by themselves and are followed by an exclamation mark.

EXAMPLES: Ugh! Help! Look Out! Hurrah! Ouch!

INTRANSITIVE VERB (VI): This VERB merely indicates existence. It does not need a direct object (DO) to complete its meaning.

              S   V   PP

EXAMPLE: The boy fished (in the stream). *Fished* is the INTRANSITIVE VERB.

LINKING VERBS: These VERBS link the COMPLEMENT to the SUBJECT in a sentence.

The VERBS *am*, *is*, *are*, *was*, *were*, *be*, *being*, *been* are forms of the VERB *be*. These *be* VERBS may also be used as HELPING VERBS.

THIS IS IMPORTANT: The verbs taste, feel, smell, sound, look, appear, become, seem, grow, remain, or stay may be used as ACTION VERBS as well as LINKING VERBS.

                S   LV   PA   PP

EXAMPLE #1: <u>Augusta</u> looks [pretty] (in that dress). Here *looks* is used as a LINKING VERB that links the ADJECTIVE *pretty* to the subject *Augusta*.

                S   VI   PP

EXAMPLE #2: <u>Augusta</u> looks (for stylish dresses). Here *looks* is used as an INTRANSITIVE VERB, for it performs the ACTION of the VERB *look* and it does not need a direct object (DO) to complete its meaning.

MNEMONIC: Mnemosyne was the goddess of memory in Greek mythology. The first "M" in the word is silent, so this word is pronounced *nemonic*. Any time you devise a memory hook to help you in studying for a test, you are using a *mnemonic*.

Suppose you are asked to memorize the names of the Great Lakes. If you remember the word *HOMES*, this memory hook will help you to remember the following: <u>H</u>uron, <u>O</u>ntario, <u>M</u>ichigan, <u>E</u>rie, and <u>S</u>uperior. As a matter of fact, someone has even devised a sentence for remembering how to spell *mnemonic*: **M**emory **N**eeds **E**very **M**ethod **O**f **N**ourishing **I**ts **C**apacity.

    The major mnemonic devices, or memory hooks, that we use in *The King's English* are Flip Flops (FL/FL) in learning the basics of parsing and OLIVIA in learning the three types of verbs. They seem to make life in Grammarland simpler.

NOUN: A NOUN is the name of a person, place, thing, or idea. A NOUN generally functions as the SUBJECT or the OBJECT of a sentence. A COMMON NOUN does not start with a capital letter; a PROPER NOUN is always capitalized.

OBJECTIVE COMPLEMENT (OC): An OBJECTIVE COMPLEMENT completes the meaning of the DIRECT OBJECT in a sentence with an ACTION VERB. It may appear either as a NOUN or ADJECTIVE.

        S   AV   DO   OC [N]   PP
EXAMPLE: We elected [Joseph] {president} (of our class).

        S   AV   DO   OC [ADJ]   PP
EXAMPLE: We consider [Joseph] {competent} (for the task).

NOTICE: In the OBJECTIVE COMPLEMENT NOUN (OC [N]) sentence, "President Joseph" *renames* the complement.

In the OBJECTIVE COMPLEMENT ADJECTIVE (OC [ADJ]) sentence, "competent Joseph" *describes* the complement.

PARSE: From the Latin *pars*, meaning "parts". (Think about *parsley*; a sprig of parsley is made up of many small parts.) In the same way the English sentence can be broken down into smaller parts by using marks and abbreviations in order to discover the relationship of every word in the sentence to every other word.

BASIC LABELS USED FOR PARSING IN *THE KING'S ENGLISH*:
1. The VERB and its helpers: Mark in green or underline twice.
2. The Subject: Underline once. _____
3. The Complement: Bracket. [ ]
4. Prepositional Phrases: Parenthesize. ( )
5. Objective Complements: Use Fancy Brackets. { }
6. Indirect Objects: Use Fancy Brackets { }

PARTICIPLES: VERBALS that end in *ing* in the present tense or end in -d, -ed, -t, or -en in the past tense. They can serve as a NOUN, ADJECTIVE, or ADVERB.

EXAMPLES:

1. The VERBAL NOUN: *Swimming* is a good exercise. (*Swimming* is a PARTICIPLE serving as a NOUN subject of the sentence.)

2. The VERBAL ADJECTIVE: I discarded the *burnt* toast.
(*Burnt* is a PARTICIPLE serving as an ADJECTIVE modifying *toast*.)

3. The VERBAL ADVERB: The bus driver stopped *to ask* directions.
(*to ask* serves as an ADVERB telling us *why* the bus driver stopped.

THE PHRASE: A PHRASE is a group of two (or more) related words that act as a single unit in a sentence. You will *never* find a SUBJECT or a VERB in a phrase; it is simply a group of words that belong together.

While a PHRASE *never* has a SUBJECT and a VERB, a CLAUSE *always* has a SUBJECT and a VERB.

THE FIVE MAJOR KINDS OF PHRASES

1. VERB PHRASE: This phrase consists of a VERB and all its helpers. It appears on the baseline as one complete verb.

EXAMPLE: Jeremy <u>will be seeking</u> work today.

2. PREPOSITIONAL PHRASE: This phrase begins with a PREPOSTION and ends with a NOUN. ADJECTIVES may be included in the phrase.

<pre>
           S   VI   PP
</pre>
EXAMPLE: Birds fly (over the rainbow).

PREPOSITIONAL PHRASES act as ADJECTIVES or ADVERBS only. These are called ADJECTIVAL and ADVERBIAL phrases.

3. PARTICIPLE PHRASE: This phrase begins with a VERBAL. This verbal is called a PARTICIPLE, which is a VERB that serves as an ADJECTIVE. It is usually followed by a PREPOSITIONAL PHRASE.

<pre>
                S   LV ADV
</pre>
EXAMPLE: The door {leading (to the porch)} is [open].

This PARTICIPLE PHRASE {leading to the porch} answers the question "which door?" It modifies the word *door*; it is a VERBAL ADJECTIVE.

4. INFINITIVE PHRASE: This phrase consists of *to* plus a VERB and acts as a VERBAL NOUN in the sentence.

EXAMPLES:

1. <u>To walk</u> was a pleasure. (Subject-VERBAL NOUN)
2. Alyssa began [to open] the box. (Direct Object-VERBAL NOUN)
3. Her wish was [to see] her brother. (Complement-VERBAL NOUN)
4. He was (about <u>to leave</u>). (Object of Preposition-VERBAL NOUN)
5. GERUND PHRASE: This phrase consists of a VERB plus *ing* and acts as a NOUN in the sentence.

EXAMPLES:

    S   LV   DO
1. <u>Walking</u> is a [pleasure]. (SUBJECT)

    S   AV   DO
2. <u>Alyssa</u> began [opening the box]. (DIRECT OBJECT)

    S   LV   PN
3. Her <u>joy</u> was [seeing her brother]. (PREDICATE NOUN)

    S   VI   PP
4. He talks (about joining the marines). (OBJECT OF THE PREPOSITION)

PREDICATE: This word comes from the Latin *praedicat*, meaning to *proclaim*. What it proclaims is very important; it proclaims what the sentence is about. When we diagram, we see that the PREDICATE includes every word that we place on the baseline except the subject.

HERE ARE THE PARTS OF THE SENTENCE THAT MAY BE INCLUDED IN THE PREDICATE:

The PREDICATE may include the VERB, the DIRECT OBJECT, the INDIRECT OBJECT, the PREDICATE NOUN, the PREDICATE ADJECTIVE, the OBJECTIVE COMPLEMENT (NOUN), or the OBJECTIVE COMPLEMENT (ADJECTIVE).

PREDICATE ADJECTIVE: An ADJECTIVE that *completes* and *describes* the subject and follows a LINKING VERB.

EXAMPLE: Candy is sweet. (The ADJECTIVE *sweet completes* the thought and *describes* the NOUN *candy*).

PREDICATE NOUN: A NOUN that *completes* and *renames* the subject and follows a LINKING VERB. EXAMPLE: Josiah is the King. (The NOUN *King completes* the thought and *renames* the NOUN *Josiah*.)

PRONOUN: A PRONOUN takes the place of a NOUN. There are six kinds of PRONOUNS.

1. Personal: (these point out a person): I, me, mine, us, ours, he, she, it, they, them.
2. Interrogative (these ask a question): who, whom, whose, which, what.
3. Demonstrative (these point out a noun): this, that, these.
4. Indefinite (these point out indefinite persons or things): each, either, one, anybody, some, more, all.
5. Compound (these combine with <u>self</u> or selves): myself, ourselves, yourself, herself, itself, oneself, themselves.
6. Relative (these show how dependent clauses relate to the independent clauses in a sentence): who, whose, whom, which, that.

PREPOSITIONS: A PREPOSITION shows how a NOUN or a PRONOUN is related to another part of the sentence. An easy way to find a PREPOSITION is to think of this sentence: The cat went ___?___ the box. Any word that you can fit into the blank is a preposition. Here are a few: about, above, across, after, around, at, before, behind, beneath, down, from, into, near, over, toward, upon, with, within, without.

Here are some exceptions to this rule: but, during, except, since, until.

A PREPOSITIONAL PHRASE consists of a PREPOSITION at the beginning, a NOUN or PRONOUN at the end, and one or more modifiers (ADJECTIVES) in the middle. EXAMPLES: (Under the bridge,) (around the corner,) (into the woods.)

REMEMBER: A **PREPOSITIONAL PHRASE** will always act as one of the following:

1. An **ADJECTIVE** (appearing underneath and modifying a **NOUN** or **PRONOUN** in the diagram.)

2. An **ADVERB** (appearing underneath and modifying a **VERB, ADJECTIVE,** or another **ADVERB** in the diagram.)

TRANSITIVE VERB: This **VERB** must have an object to complete the thought. The very word *transitive* carries the idea of completion. Think of Trans World Airlines that circles the globe, or think of the Trans Canada Highway that goes from one end of Canada to the other.

VERB COMPLEMENTS act either as **DIRECT OBJECTS** (DO) or **INDIRECT OBJECTS** (IO). These *complete the thought of the sentence.*

ONE LAST WORD:

GLOSSARY: This word comes from the Latin *glossa*, which means *a word requiring explanation*. Webster defines glossary as "a list of words with their definitions, often found at the back of a book." I hope you enjoy our glossary and use it often!

"He who forgets the language of gratitude
will never be on speaking terms with happiness."
- C. Neil Strait (1934-2003)

The King's English copyright 2015
Cover Design by Lori Yatron, *Living Word Calligraphy*
*Contact us at thecolorofenglish@gmail.com or
bgdandme@comcast.net*

CPSIA information can be obtained at www.ICGtesting.com
Printed in the USA
BVOW10s2202180116

433369BV00006BA/130/P